PERFORMANCE
anxiety

A Memoir By
JACKIE McCOWN

PERFORMANCE
anxiety

Life After Sexual Abuse
A Story of Brokenness,
Redemption, and *freedom*

Anchorage, Alaska

PERFORMANCE *anxiety*
© 2021 Jackie McCown.

All rights reserved. No part of this publication may be reproduced, distributed, or transmitted in any form or by any means, including photocopying, recording, or other electronic or mechanical methods, without the prior written permission of the publisher, except in the case of brief quotations embodied in critical reviews and certain other noncommercial uses permitted by copyright law. For permission requests, please contact the author.

Published by Jackie McCown | Anchorage, AK
ISBN (Print): 978-1-7373703-0-7
ISBN (Kindle): 978-1-7373703-1-4
Library of Congress Control Number (LCCN): 2021911451
Printed in the United States of America
Prepared for Publication: www.wendykwalters.com

DISCLAIMER

To protect the innocent and the guilty, some names and descriptive details about people have been changed. The events in this story are presented through the filter of the author's memory and experiences. She shares her story as she remembers it to help herself heal and offer a path of healing to others on their journey.

To contact the author:

Dedication

To Jock "Coach" Ambrose

For seeing what could be and providing hope and encouragement. For my life. For so many lives.

TCTCG!

PERFORMANCE *anxiety*

PERFORMANCE *anxiety*

Praise for Performance Anxiety

In a world often framed by the term "anxiety" Jackie has allowed heaven to take her heart and wrap it around the incredible kindness of the word.

Anxiety and Performance became her protect. Humor her guardian. High intelligence her entrance. Perception of good was her ticket to breath. Albeit staccato for decades.

Over the years of an ordinary life as a daughter and a wife and a friend and a mom she edged her way into intimacy with the legitimate extraordinaries of herself. Her legacy of history and the one shaping ahead of her. Her profound and unique color of brave.

When Jackie wrote these words she loaned her braves and her afraids to anyone willing to read the testify. She speaks with a tremor and a determine. It is raw. It is real. It is pragmatic. It is dichotomous.

And it is a mighty Pray.

Anyone—no matter the affiliation with PTSD—would be bettered for the reading.

—LISA JENNETT

Author of *When I Last Saw Me*, Accidentally Successful Entrepreneur

Performance Anxiety is not another story to find "interesting." Jackie McCown's provocative and creative rendering of her story will spur you to do something as a result of the reading—dig deeper, love fuller, maybe get up one more time. Whether this is your exact experience or not, there is enough humanity in it to change you. This is the every-woman, pour-another-one, clip-your-hair-up-and-get-comfortable book. Jackie is that friend who tells the truth—hers and yours—without blaming or excusing or adapting the facts to a level of comfort that looks polite but is only a lie with lipstick. You need her voice and you need her to help you find yours.

—PAIGE CORLEY HENDERSON
Co-Founder of Fellowship of the Sword, Author of *The Genesis Girls* Series

This is an uplifting story of one woman's journey: how a life in a pain-filled downward spiral was transformed by God's love, and ultimately healed. The author has found her voice, and it is a strong one.

—MARY HOOVER
Attorney, Friend

Jackie gives the reader a gift by sharing a story that many will be able to relate to on various levels from many different perspectives. That connection to hurts, challenges, abuse, faults and even superior abilities such as swimming isn't her ultimate point, however. She walks you to more and better; freedom from what may hold you back and permission to live fully.

—SCOTT PRICKETT
Author of *Transforming the Prodigal Soul*

Performance Anxiety is an "I once was lost but now I'm found" anthem that rings so true it is simultaneously comforting and unsettling. Those who have suffered sexual abuse respond in a myriad of ways, usually unhealthy, often manifesting as destructive patterns over which they struggle to gain control without understanding the root cause. Jackie gets to the root. With loving vulnerability and tender transparency,

PERFORMANCE *anxiety*

she finds her voice. As she sings her freedom anthem—first in shy, halting tones, then in clear resounding brave crescendo—she invites all abuse victims everywhere to harmonize their story with hers and join heaven's joyous victorious choir—let freedom ring!

—WENDY K. WALTERS

Writing & Publishing Coach, Author, Editor, Ghostwriter, "Fwendy"

A Word from Jackie's Mom

My daughter, my friend. As difficult as it was to learn your story, I am so proud of you that you found your voice and the courage to tell that story. I love you to infinity and more—I've been truly blessed that God gave you to me.

—Carol Wiersma

Acknowledgments

Hey Mac.

Thank you. No. Really. Thank you. Oodles and bunches. For loving me through the brokenness. For being my Mac. You really are the bestest Mac ever. Juice. Jackson.

For Lisa.

Thank you for seeing me and speaking life and truth. The blood of the lamb and …

A huge shout out to my A-team.

Coffee. Wine. And—maybe—a little more wine. Because Jesus juice. Thanks for going through this thing called life with me and never, ever letting me forget I am enough.

PERFORMANCE *anxiety*

Contents

15   *chapter one*
LIFE AFTER

17   *chapter two*
WIERSMAS DON'T MAKE MISTAKES

35   *chapter three*
THE LIES SHE BELIEVED

55   *chapter four*
PATTERNS

69   *chapter five*
NATIONALS

77   *chapter six*
ESCAPE

93   *chapter seven*
IT ALL COMES CRASHING DOWN

101   *chapter eight*
TURN THE PAGE

107   *chapter nine*
SURFACING

117   *chapter ten*
GRACE TO HEAL

137   *chapter eleven*
LOVE THEM ANYWAY

151   *chapter twelve*
WALKING IN FREEDOM

161   *photo gallery*

169   *about the author*
JACKIE MCCOWN

PERFORMANCE *anxiety*

chapter one

LIFE AFTER

Healing from trauma can also mean strength and joy. The goal of healing is not a papering-over of changes in an effort to preserve or present things as normal. It is to acknowledge and wear your new life—warts, wisdom, and all—with courage.

CATHERINE WOODIWISS

I've been where you are, at least bits and parts. The darkness. The hiding. The self-protection. And, unless you know me well, you'd probably never suspect. Most people are surprised to learn I was diagnosed with MS in 2001. "But you look so good," is the comment I receive most often. If I'm living in such a way that you can't tell I have a debilitating autoimmune disease, imagine the surprise when I share that I am also a survivor of both childhood and adult sexual abuse.

For decades I kept quiet about the trauma I'd experienced. My voice didn't exist because I didn't know what to say or to whom. I was hiding, as the saying goes, "in plain sight." I was always "happy." I "didn't know a stranger." I was "one of the girls." But I wasn't. And everything I wanted to scream out loud was pushed deeper and deeper, locked safely inside. Until it wasn't. But that's for later. For now, I just want to talk to you. I want to say to you all the things I wish someone had said to me. Hopefully, by telling my story, I can give you a safe space to tell yours.

What I want to tell you is that I'm sorry.

I'm sorry you were hurt.

I am sorry for the hurt that is still with you.

I'm sorry you were not protected.

I. Am. Sorry.

I want to look into your eyes and hold you there. Let the truth be seen when so many others looked past you and the hurt you have hidden. I want to hug you. Tight.

I want to hold you until the tears come. And go.

I want to be with you until you are ready to be alone again.

I will tell you over and over again how much my heart hurts for you. And, when you are ready, I will look at you again and see you— really see you. And I will share my smile because that is all I can do.

Your pain isn't my pain, but we can walk through the pain together.

And on the other side, we can find grace and peace and mercy and comfort. And, maybe just maybe, forgiveness.

chapter two

WIERSMAS DON'T MAKE MISTAKES

Most fears of rejection rest on the desire for approval from other people.
HARVEY MACKAY

"We've been looking everywhere for you!" my dad bellowed. "Do you have any idea how worried your mom and I have been?!"

"I'm sorry," I replied. "I was just down at Leah's house. We were in the basement playing. I tried to call a few times, but the line was always busy."

"That is no excuse. You know what time you have to be home. You don't just stay at your friend's because the phone line is busy."

Daddy was unhappy. Really unhappy.

"I'm sorry," I offered sheepishly.

"Well, sorry isn't enough. It is not okay for you to worry us like that. It is *not* okay! You will go to your room, and you will not have dinner tonight."

PERFORMANCE *anxiety*

I am beyond confused. And afraid. *I was only down at Leah's. Mom knew I was playing with her. Mom **knew** … Now I don't get dinner???*

"But Daddy, I tried to call. I really did," I pleaded. "And I was just down at Leah's, and mom knew where I was and …"

"That," my father insisted, "is not okay. It is not okay to worry us like that. That is not how we behave. That is not the right way to do things. That is not my way. That is not God's way. Children do not worry their parents like that." He paused a terrible pause. My head went down in the dread of shame. I held my breath, waiting. "Now, go to your room," he dismissed me.

Tears filled my eyes as I walked to my room. I really truly did not understand. I'd done something to upset my mom and dad and God … I was not a good daughter.

⊱ ☙ ❧ ☙ ❧ ⊰

The plate slipped from my hands, wet from cleaning it completely before putting it in the dishwasher. Its pieces warned me of the mistake I'd made. I could feel her eyes on me even before I heard her words.

"Be careful!" my mom scolded. Her words echoed her frown. "Don't be in such a hurry."

"You need to take care of the things we have," dad added. "We take our time and take care of what we have because we are good stewards of what God's given us."

"I'm sorry. I didn't mean to break it. I'll do better next time," I said penitently.

"Of course you will," my dad offered encouragement, "we just have to remember to do things the right way."

WIERSMAS DON'T MAKE MISTAKES

The right way. There was always a right way. And the right way almost always centered on life at my father's military school.

"When I was at St. John's, we made our beds with hospital corners. Always neat. You had better be able to bounce a quarter off your bed. If you didn't do things the right way, you'd be walking the guard path. No matter how hot or how cold, you did it the right way, or you walked the path." These were regular reminders my dad often remembered aloud for me to take the lesson. His soundtrack became my own.

≤∽ ⋄⋆⋄⋆⋄ ∽≥

"You have nice things," my father's baritone voice scolded. "We spend good money on making sure you have nice things, and this is how you take care of them?"

My eyes fell to the yellow hardwood of my bedroom floor.

"It is not acceptable for you to just shove good, clean clothes into your dresser." His voice conveyed his disappointment and anger.

Each drawer was opened in turn. Clothes that I thought I'd put away well enough tumbled to the floor as my dad dumped them out.

"Okay," I mumbled softly.

Finally, the bottom drawer was emptied, and the full 6' 2" frame of my father stood guard.

"You will refold every one of these and put them away correctly. Do you understand me?" he warned, brow furrowed, eyes forcing me to do anything but look at him.

"Okay. Yes." Inside I shrank away from the mess on the floor. The disappointment in his voice wounded my fragile heart. All I ever wanted to do was please him—but I never seemed able to come up to the mark.

"Good. Remember, there is *one* right way," his words reverberated as he turned and walked out of my room.

I can still remember my father's words with piercing clarity. These words aligned with an innate understanding I'd had from my earliest childhood—***Wiersmas didn't make mistakes.***

Wiersmas did everything exceedingly well.

Wiersmas knew what to do, when to do it, and how to do it.

There was no compromise.

There was no room for questioning or individual opinions.

Things were the way they were. Period.

As much as my childhood was filled with immense love from my parents, the demons of generational abuse filtered through these communications. What they meant by them didn't matter nearly so much as how they landed on my impressionable soul. These impossible expectations wrapped around every core memory, shadowing them with the knowledge that I was not quite good enough to be a member of the Wiersma family. Not enough. I needed to try harder and do better if I was going to be accepted.

I needed to try harder and do better if I was going to be accepted

It wasn't until well into adulthood that I learned about the abuse my father suffered at the hands of his father. Fortunately for my father, he escaped the harshest hand at home by attending a prestigious military boarding school. The perfection required at home transferred well to the demands of an intense army regimen at school. Although safe there from his father's rage, my dad learned an equally strict manner of walking through life. Performance translated to success, success to promotion. Promotion meant honor, and honor filled the emotional void at home. If my father could find love, it would be in proving his worth. In being the best.

I wish I had known this about him earlier. I wish he had confronted this in himself before hopelessly locked into a destructive pattern that repeated itself.

Abuse often takes different forms from generation to generation, and I did not suffer the same mental and physical harm as my father. However, the lessons he learned, lessons of perfection and performance and single-mindedness, certainly were front and center in my life. I understood from a very young age that mistakes were not acceptable. Doing the "right" thing the "right" way was the benchmark across the board.

∽ⳍⳍⳍ∽

Coffee Tuesdays. I loved coffee Tuesdays! The moms were all at Nan's drinking their coffee. All of us kids were outside enjoying the fresh air. Matt and Blair took off on their bikes, leading the way on our latest adventure. No way was I going to let them get that far ahead of me! I pulled the rubber covers with their sparkling streamers off the handlebars, pushed hard on the pavement to give myself a solid start, and pedaled as hard as I could to catch them. The harder they pedaled, the closer I got. I was good at riding bikes. I had long legs—strong legs—and it wasn't long before I caught and passed them.

As soon as we got to the end of the street, we turned around, racing back to our starting point. Lucky for us, there was no traffic on the street today. We could ride anywhere in the road, passing back and forth, moving left and right to block each other. It was such a great game. The wind blew my hair into a frenzy. The tires rolled—tsk, tsk, tsk—the playing cards taped to the spokes keeping time with my speed. My eyes teared in the wind as I raced to the finish. I was going to win. I was winning. I smiled an all-encompassing smile as I got to Nan's house, slammed on my brakes, and waited for the others to finish.

"That. Is how. You win. A race," I panted.

"Well, that's only the first race," Matt challenged, turning his bike around to go again.

We all lined up across the street. Round two. I would not be defeated.

"On your marks. Get set. Go!" Blair shouted.

I pushed off with all my might, practically jumping out of the banana seat of the absolute best, fastest, pinkest bike ever. I ruled the block on my bike. I put both feet up on the pedals. I lowered my shoulders, crouching into speed-demon position, scraping my chin on the rough metal, now exposed from removing the streamered handgrips. *Forward*, I commanded my bike. *Faster*, I demanded of my legs. Without understanding, I noticed that my chin hurt. I ignored the pain, though; there is a race to win. The pain, however, would not let go.

I dragged the back of my right hand across my chin. Stupid chin. As I reached out to grab the handlebars, I saw bright red blood on my hand. It took a moment for it to register. The pain. The blood. *What the heck?!*

I stopped pedaling. Somehow my kindergarten self knew pain and blood and bicycles don't go together. Somehow, I knew, "This is not okay." I turned my bike around and rode back to Nan's house. I had to get to my mom. *What had I done? What had I done?!!!*

I dropped my bike in the yard (that was not acceptable). I raced into the house without knocking (that was not acceptable). I ran into the kitchen, interrupting all the moms enjoying their coffee (that was not acceptable). I was bleeding (that was not acceptable).

Mom pulled me close, hugging me, before taking a closer look at what had made me so upset.

"Could I have a towel?" she asked Nan.

Sitting on my mom's lap, towel held to my chin, I tried not to cry. *Wiersmas were brave.* I had to be brave.

"Looks like we'll need to go to the ER," my mom announced. *I had done something wrong. I had done something bad. Daddy would **not** be happy. I'd gone and hurt myself instead of winning the stupid bike race.* I didn't even know how I'd done it, but there you had it. I had messed up. Again.

The trip to the hospital was a blur. Getting the local anesthetic and the stitches was a blur. Leaving the hospital was a blur. Driving to go see my dad at the garage, however, crystal clear. I am afraid—afraid to tell my dad what I've done. I cannot tell my mom I am afraid. I cannot admit to the fear. I must shove it down, keep it quiet, keep me quiet. *Children are to be seen and not heard.* I will not make a sound.

No matter how quiet I was on the outside, I was screaming inside. I was certain my dad would not be happy with me. *He is such a large man. He is such a powerful man. I don't like making him unhappy.* It is scary.

When we finally arrived at the garage where my dad's race car was kept, there was a frenzy of familiar faces and loud noises and a lot of, well, not calm. The apparent chaos only added to my fear. Everything seemed out of control, just like me, just like hurting myself and needing stitches. Out of control is not something we do. I am even more frightened. *Daddy is going to be so angry*, I think … except he isn't.

My father wasn't angry. He hugged me. His eyes were full of concern.

"Hi, Crash," he smiled. "Well now, that's not so bad. Are you okay?" He embraced me. He cradled me.

I felt confused. *Why isn't he angry? He's supposed to be angry. I messed up. I didn't do the race well. I hurt myself, and I lost the race. No, I quit the race. Wiersmas* **don't** *quit. He has to be upset. He has to.*

But daddy wasn't angry. He was smiling. He was joking. "Did you just call me Crash?" I looked up at him in wonder. *This is funny???*

A daring and perhaps accident-prone child, I remember being afraid to tell my father I'd fallen on my bike and gotten stitches in my face. For the life of me, I cannot tell you why I was afraid, but I was. I knew deep down inside I had done something wrong. I knew my father would be disappointed in me. He wasn't, but the groundwork for how I saw the world had obviously already been laid by that point. I was five.

≈☙☙☙≈

People are often perplexed when I share that I felt worthless or questioned my value within my family at such a young age. By all appearances, we had a wonderful, loving family dynamic. And we did … except. Buried abuses from my father's childhood and denominational teachings from my family's Christian Reformed church paved a harsh and narrow road for life. Adding to this family dynamic, my parents, out of an abundance of love, adopted two children when I was six. He was nine. She was eight. They came from a horribly broken environment, but a closed adoption meant my parents didn't have any idea what that entailed. What it meant for me was that an idyllic childhood ended. My place was usurped, and decades of abuse began.

My abuse began with a look of pride—the look upon the face of a parent or grandparent that elicits confidence. We learn it from infancy. The look gives us the calm assurance we are wanted, encouraged, and a basis for joy. Each of us knows that smile, nod, embrace. It says, "Well done, my child."

I saw that look, the unmistakable pride on my grandfather's face, as he stood at the door with *them*. Two strangers. My grandfather, the patriarch—Charlie (Chuck), introduced me to *his* new grand*son*.

"Jackie, this is your brother, John," my Grandfather beamed.

What? I thought. My brother?

"Hi," I whispered.

"Hi," John replied.

He looks like me. How can he look like me? John's blonde hair and blue eyes were eerily familiar. The afternoon sun illuminated the highlights in his hair, and he looked like an angelic boy version of me.

"And," Grandpa offered in passing, "this is Dori." There was a tangible difference in how my grandfather presented the children.

Though biological siblings, Dori's flat brown hair and green eyes stood out in marked contrast to John's lighter features.

How can she be his sister? I wondered. *They don't look anything alike.*

"Well, John," grandpa smiled as he turned and put his hand on John's back. "How about we all go in?"

The new boy had taken grandpa's name as his own. John Charles. My grandfather's son now had a son. The heir. At long last someone who could carry on the Wiersma family name.

I, a daughter, was not an heir. Loved, but not someone to carry on the family name. That position of honor and responsibility was displayed for all the world to see, and Dori, wrecked by her early childhood, must have known her place was not as honored as his was as well. She must have seen and felt her brother elevated in this new family, leaving her to wonder how she fit in. To make matters worse, she must have known that she certainly fell behind me in the order of things. True, I was not a boy, so behind John, but I was the naturally born child, so of course, I was next in the lineup for approval and affection.

Dori let me know her disdain for me and her new life from week one.

"Mom," I called, "Have you seen my yellow duck?"

"No, honey, I haven't. Have you looked under your bed?" mom called back.

"I did. He isn't here. I can't find him!" my voice rose as I began to panic.

"I'm sure he's in your room somewhere. He was there last night when you went to bed."

Mom's confidence calmed me as she stood in my doorway. "But Mom …" I protested, my renewed searching proved fruitless. "He isn't in here. Anywhere." Tears rolled down my flushed cheeks. My beloved yellow duck was missing!

"I'm sure we'll find him," she hugged me.

The doorbell rang and interrupted our search.

"Oh, hi Cindy," mom's cheerful voice called out for me to hear.

My best friend and neighbor, Cindy, had come to play. The yellow duck was forgotten—for the moment, that is.

≼ ଓଔଓ ≽

"Jackie?" mom asked, "What happened to your doorknob?"

I had the coolest doorknob cover. It had little scented balls in it. It made my room smell all pretty and pink and girly.

"Nothing," I answered. My doorknob was just fine when I'd left my room that morning.

"Jackie," she encouraged, "It's okay. You can tell me."

"Tell you what?"

"Jackie. You need to tell me what happened to your doorknob,"

"Nothing. Nothing happened."

"Be truthful," mom encouraged an answer.

"Mom. I don't know. Nothing happened."

Mom's face was angry now, "Well, someone did something. You can tell me. Just tell the truth, and it will be alright."

"But I didn't do anything," I pleaded.

"Hmm. Well, stay here in your room until I come back then." And with that, she turned and walked out of my room, closing the door behind her.

"Dori …" my mom called.

I don't know what conversation my mom had with Dori, but within a few minutes, Dori had bolted through my bedroom door shouting, "You are so stupid!"

PERFORMANCE *anxiety*

Her hate-filled eyes glared at me, and she yelled again, "You are **so, so** stupid! You **do not** tell on me. I didn't break your stupid doorknob. You can't prove that I did! You are so spoiled and so stupid! Who even needs a dumb, smelly doorknob anyway!!!"

Things between Dori and me were never on solid footing. I knew she hated me. I didn't care for her either, and our tenuous relationship went from dubious to disastrous.

> *... our tenuous relationship went from dubious to disastrous*

Toys were stolen. Lies were told to cover up the thievery. Items were broken. Anger-filled responses met every question or comment or direction. Sharing with me was not part of Dori's game. She hated me for who I was and used words to communicate that message at every turn. Where I'd once struggled internally to meet the demands of my parents to ensure their approval and love, I now found myself verbally assaulted at every turn. I simply couldn't understand why she hated me so very much. I put more and more effort into trying to understand how and what she needed so I could perform well enough for her.

John joined in the abuse shortly after Dori. Perhaps it was weeks or even months, but the two found their bond in tormenting me. Any game we played ended with me losing or being left behind.

I heard them laughing. They were in the bedroom hallway. I knew what that meant. In moments they came racing down the hall, "Time for a Jackie sack!" they shouted. John grabbed me around the waist while Dori slipped the sleeping bag over my head.

"Stop it!" I screamed, muffled by the bag. I struggled to get free, but I was no match for John's strength.

"Going down!" he shouted as he pushed me, wriggling, to the ground. Dori pulled the bag all the way down to my feet. I couldn't breathe. I was sweating; panic filled me. I **knew** what came next.

"Woo-hoo!" they shouted in chorus, and I went sliding down the stairs, head first. Bump, bump, bump … I didn't say a word. I knew this game. I tried to count the stairs, bracing myself for the hard, brick fireplace hearth at the bottom. Thud! My head hit hard, barely cushioned by the sleeping bag "fluff." I lay still, hoping that was the end of it. It was. The moment I hit the bottom, they were off to play something else. I wriggled my way out of the bag, hot tears streaming down my face, my hair standing up from the static.

I wanted to tell on them. I almost did. But instead, I hugged my knees to my chest and rocked back and forth. *What have I done?* I wondered. *Why don't they like me? Why am I not good enough?* Sobs shook my little body. I hoped my mom would walk through and notice. In my mind, she swooped me up, hugged me close, then scolded John and Dori. That never happened. I was alone. Bruised. Confused. No idea how to make it stop. Miserable.

Why, when I was doing everything I could to learn what they needed from me and do those things well, did they treat me so badly? What had I done? Why was I not good enough? Performing well and to expectation had always brought me love and approval in the past. This new game with these new people plagued me.

~∞∞∞~

I never said anything, no matter how many times it happened. I wanted to, of course, but I didn't think I could. I know it seems strange, but John was a boy—the heir—and I was just a girl. Dori was older than me, and they had picked her. I could almost understand why they would pick a boy, but why did they need another girl? *I must not have been good enough,* was a constant thought in the back of my mind, but I couldn't risk becoming a problem child too—a whiner. My family did not like complainers. They didn't like a tattletale. Tears were much more likely to be met with, "Toughen up," than a comforting cuddle.

"But why didn't you say something?" I am often asked. It seems so perfectly obvious to me. John was a boy, the heir, and I was not. It was drilled into me that children were to be seen and not heard. Children were not supposed to complain. John and Dori were changing the game I had to play, and I had yet to perfect that game. Although I cannot recollect my parents struggling with John and Dori at this point, I knew definitively that I could not, under any circumstance, add to my parents' burden. I had to be the good child, and grumbling was certainly not part of that performance. Besides, my parents had chosen these two—the others—and who would I be to upset the dynamic my parents had put into place. After all, no one had chosen me.

"Because of you, your mommy almost died," the words echoed in my soul. I must have done something very bad. Bad enough they needed other children to make up for it. What I didn't know until well into my 40s was that I was a miracle baby. My mother was never supposed to be able to have children. She hemorrhaged weeks after giving birth to me and survived thanks to God and some quick-acting doctors. My parents had always dreamt of a large family and were grateful to have me. Grateful my mom survived. But just as we never really talked about sex in our family, neither did I ever hear about my mom's pregnancy or my birth. Except to be reminded, "Your mom almost died when you were born." Details, left out, often write a very different story in the mind of a child.

WIERSMAS DON'T MAKE MISTAKES

※ ରେ ରେ ରେ ※

In addition to the challenges of life with John and Dori, I was also in pain. Literal physical pain. Many months and doctor's visits later, I was diagnosed with juvenile rheumatoid arthritis. I had only 40% mobility from my hips down to my toes. Blood draws hurt. My hips hurt. The medicines they made me take tasted terrible. I couldn't escape my siblings' cruelty, and now I was trapped in a body that tortured me too. I am told, despite the pain, I was always a happy child. I wonder now how much of that was innate happiness and how much was part of my performance.

Still, I consistently heard, "Jackie's always been a happy kid." Teachers, parents of friends, aunts, and uncles always complimented me for being a happy child. Whenever anyone said it, my parents beamed with pride. "She's a trooper, alright," daddy would pat my head. I knew he was proud of me for not crying when they did a blood draw. If I smiled through pain and didn't complain, it made daddy proud. *Wiersmas were strong.* I could play strong. I could perform happy if it meant approval.

If I smiled through pain and didn't complain, it made daddy proud

The doctors told my parents the best thing they could do for me was to move to a warm, dry climate. In a loving yet extremely challenging decision, my parents moved us from the familiarity and support of extended family and their hometown to Scottsdale, Arizona. My aching, tired body convalesced in the dry heat of the Arizona desert. Pain decreased, and mobility increased. Slowly but surely, I regained my physical well-being. The emotional decline caused by John and Dori, unfortunately, did not improve.

PERFORMANCE *anxiety*

"She won't even swear," John and Dori taunted as we walked down the middle of the street with our neighborhood friends.

Their challenge struck me. We *did not* swear. It was not something good Christians did. It was not something a Wiersma did. It was not part of performing well to the expected standard. And yet ... here were my brother and sister, who obviously knew so much more than me and were so much more valuable than me, pushing me to do what they said I could not. I would show them.

"Shit," I said with loud clarity.

They laughed. All of them. John. Dori. Their friends. I had made them laugh. I had done well. I would be more ardent in watching and listening for ways to make them so happy they would laugh. I would focus my energy, on pins and needles, anxiously seeking ways to make my parents happy, my siblings happy, everyone happy. Then I would be good enough.

John and Dori and their friends began to include me in more and more things. My newfound position bolstered my efforts. I began to understand their needs and wants and how to make sure I was included. I would do what they asked, when they asked, the way they asked.

When John asked me to join him and the neighbor boys in their camper one summer day, I didn't hesitate. I wasn't afraid. I was just going to hang out with them. I was included. When he asked me to sit on the bed of the foldout camper, I didn't suspect. I was included. When he told me to remove my shorts and panties, I felt funny, but I trusted that he wouldn't ask me to do anything bad. He was my brother. He was the chosen one, the heir. I was included, after all.

Now I understand some young boys and girls play show and tell. They learn about one another's body parts in secret and without malice.

I'm also aware that both kiddos involved are in agreement with what's happening. It is, as much as it can be, innocent exploration. That was not the case with me. As I sat in that camper, giving my best to make sure they would still include me, I knew something was wrong. God forbid I say anything, protest in any way. The only thing I could think to do was to ask that John and his friends pull the curtain separating the bed from the rest of the camper, so I didn't have to see their faces. I essentially hid my face. The shame covered me, and I hid, but I still performed.

The camper incident never happened again, apparent curiosity satisfied. The emotional and verbal abuse continued with consistency and intensity. Words I'd never heard barraged my ears. Anger flowed out of Dori toward me, and I learned to cower. I learned to withdraw. I learned what I needed to do to stay off her radar. As much as I was learning what I needed to do to be included with John, I was just as quickly learning what I needed to do to stay as far away from Dori as possible.

~ ☙ ❧ ☙ ~

Now that I think about it, I was set up from the start. My family and my church were at odds with one another, and they didn't even know it. On the one hand, the Christian Reformed church we attended taught me I was worthless on my own. The only hope for any of us was the undeserved grace of God. Heaven couldn't be earned. Good works were a lie. God either chose you or not, and you just had to hope and pray you were one of His elect.

Contrast that ideal with a family that very much insisted there was one right way for everything. At home, you either performed according to expectation, or you were wrong. You did what you were told. Affection and acceptance were contingent on "doing the right thing."

Think about that for a minute. Church says you can't perform to any good end. Home and family tell you the only way to love and acceptance is to perform correctly. *Wait. What? I can't perform, but I must perform.* It is a never-ending circle of opposition. Confusing. At best. And what it did was leave me wondering if I'd ever be good enough. Certainly, I'd never perform well enough to get to Heaven. Because you simply cannot ever do anything to get to Heaven. So, I knew from the outset I'd never be good enough.

It's a conundrum, to be sure. As I reflect upon a game I couldn't win, I begin to understand there was a significant amount of God's grace missing from my life. The church taught we were only saved by God's grace, but they didn't extend any grace. Those in power spoke of God's love for me, but were far more proficient at pointing out how wrong I was than they were showing me His love. It's a difficult thing to grow up knowing you'll never be enough. It's a difficult thing to believe you must perform and perform and perform again, only to have that countered with the truth that performing will get you nothing.

But during my childhood, God was far away somewhere. My family was near. Performing met with their approval, so I became very—very good at performing.

chapter three

THE LIES SHE BELIEVED

Just because you have a thought doesn't mean it's true.

DR. JOE DISPENZA

Fear is a liar. Its close cousin, shame, will upend even the slightest ounce of truth you can grasp. These two—fear and shame—will wreak havoc in your life with as much ferocity as you will permit for as long as you will allow. They will rewrite your entire life if you let them. Fear and shame have one goal: to keep you "less than." They will work their evil to ensure you know you are not enough and that you are even less than not enough. In the language of St. Paul, you are "the leastest." And once fear and shame have you believing that lie, they've got you. A single lie becomes the filter through which you see everything. You assume their work, lying to yourself again and again until you don't consider anything but the lies you now wholeheartedly believe.

PERFORMANCE *anxiety*

What lies do you tell yourself? We all do it. Some of us are better at hiding the lies. Some of us believe the lies so thoroughly, any other option, any other explanation of events is completely off the table. The lie becomes "your truth," and your mind will battle any evidence to the contrary.

As you will learn, I was a competitive swimmer. The pool was my sanctuary and my performance arena. I recently met with my swimming coach from Miami University. Thirty years of lie-filled life had happened between that day and the last time we saw one another. I was full of more emotion than I can give words. I had lived with the heavy weight of shame for so many years, knowing I had cost my coach and my team the victory, knowing that I had let them all down. Failed.

In the end, what I believed to be the worst moment of my swimming career, the knowledge that I had failed *everyone*, was met with kindness, gentleness, and truth.

"That's not the way I see it at all," he said. "The way I see it is that everyone did the best they could, and we were at Nationals. We were there during a time in our school's history, in our Conference's history, when people just weren't making it to Nationals. It was pretty awesome that we were even there."

∽ ☙ ☙ ☙ ∽

Childhood sexual abuse has an insidious way of re-wiring your brain. Literally. One action, one significant action, changes the way you understand the world. If perception is reality, the reality of an abuse victim is forever altered as the filter through which every single moment of life will be perceived and experienced is permanently re-wired. Truth becomes a fabrication outside the grasp of the abuse survivor. The lies of abuse become the abused's reality.

THE LIES SHE BELIEVED

LIE NUMBER ONE: SEX IS LOVE

P.D.A. Don't you just love it? No. Seriously. How many times have you seen that textbook display of affection and thought, "Get a room?" Did you, like many of my generation, grow up in a home where outward displays of affection were rare at best? Did you ever see your parents hug, embrace, or—wide-eyed, gaping—see them kiss?

Did you grow up hearing your father speak loving and adoring words to your mother? Or witness your mother telling your father how much she loved and appreciated him? Did you get a lot of hugs, or were they rarities given out on special occasions? Do you remember being told how loved you were? That you were a precious gift from God? That you were worthy of love and affection just because you were you? If you grew up in my home, that answer would be, "Probs not."

Here's the big one. Okay, maybe *a* big one and not *the* big one, but significant, nonetheless. Did one of your parents have "the talk" with you? Did someone older, wiser, with an essential role in your life tell you about your developing body? Did someone explain sex to you in an open, healthy conversation? Again, if you grew up in my generation, in my house, the answer would be a resounding, "No."

A good puritanical home, we never talked about sex. At least not in any healthy way. There were lots of "boys will be boys" jokes and off-color remarks, but nothing about appropriate physical displays of love.

> *Did someone explain sex to you in an open, healthy conversation, or were you left to figure out what was appropriate on your own?*

PERFORMANCE *anxiety*

We never discussed the biblical or biological purposes and ideals for a healthy sexual relationship.

⁂

We are wired for connection—mental, emotional, and physical. Study after study has shown that infants and young children deprived of connection are left scarred for life. "Many children who have not had ample physical and emotional attention are at higher risk for behavioral, emotional and social problems as they grow up."[1] While most children won't suffer the neglect of impoverished orphanages, lack of connection does open the door for wrong thinking and unhealthy relationships to fill the void.

When John paid attention to 6-year-old Jackie, it was mentally and physically abusive, but it was attention from a significant person in my life. Much like young children will tease someone they like in lieu of expressing their feelings directly, having John give me negative attention was still attention. It formed a connection. When his attention became sexual, it opened my eyes to an entirely new and twisted deeper connection. Once again, negative attention, whether understood or not, is better than no attention.

⁂

"You can touch it if you want to ..." he offered in such a kind, considerate way. I felt almost guilty even thinking about not touching it.

"But, but ..." I really didn't want to. This was icky. I didn't like it. *Just do it*, my obedient little girl brain insisted. *Do it and get it over with.* My thoughts raced back and forth like a ping-pong match on fast-forward. *This is so gross. This is not me. I am not doing this. Someone else is.*

"It's really okay. Nothing's wrong with it. You're okay … if you want to …" Cajoling. Encouraging. Reassuring. Physical touch instantly meant touching sexual parts, which translated to being accepted, loved. If I just did what he asked, he'd be happy with me. He'd include me. He would love me.

LIE NUMBER TWO: I CANNOT PROTECT MYSELF

Have you ever had a sore throat and the husky or almost non-existent voice that comes with it? Crazy how we try that much harder to speak, all but yelling just to force the words loud enough to be heard. Imagine if you didn't have a voice. Imagine if you lost yours.

How did I lose my voice? I'm not sure I ever had one to begin with. From earliest childhood, I understood children were to be seen and not heard. An adorable performance might be welcome—twirling in a fluffy pink dress or splashing lakeside—but speaking out of turn or in an ugly tone was met with a harsh look at best or a slap across the face at worse.

My parents were the product of their parents, and their parents were the product of their parents, you get the idea. The stern pragmatism of Dutch tradition and nose-to-the-grindstone work ethic left little room for silliness or dissent. You did what you were expected to do. Be seen, not heard. Parents were not to be questioned. Parents, after all, are the earthly representation of God himself. Who was I to question or argue with that?

PERFORMANCE *anxiety*

◈❀❀❀◈

When someone says or does something you don't like, how do you respond? Dollars to donuts, you say something. When someone hurts you, how do you react? I bet you'll say something. You may yell. You may even lash out in response, but it almost certainly is accompanied by saying something. Saying *something*—yelling, screaming is the first line of defense in self-protection.

Sexual abuse obliterates your voice. In the midst of even the most adamant, "NO," the abuse survivor understands their voice has no impact on the outcome of the situation. An immediately learned helplessness ensues. I knew my words, my voice, had no impact. I learned I could not say one single thing that would alter the situation in which I found myself. And, at a neurological level, I learned that I must remain silent and endure. The silence abuse demands is especially impactful in childhood when the understanding of relationships with others and self is not yet formed. In primary learning years, abuse teaches the child to be silent. This lesson is pervasive, potentially impacting the abuse survivor for life.

◈❀❀❀◈

You know when you get a cut, and it seems every time you turn around, you're banging it against something? Or when you bite your cheek and every other bite seems to close at that same exact place? You have a vulnerable spot; you keep hurting it without even trying. That's what being abused feels like. Better yet, that is precisely the aftermath of abuse. The wound of childhood sexual abuse limits your thinking. It halts a process in development that leaves you vulnerable. Much like bumping the same cut again and again, or biting the same spot in your mouth over and over, abuse leaves you in a loop of vulnerability.

⁓ಿಂಠಿಂಠಿಂಠಿ⁓

"Come here," John grabs my arm. My insides clench in knowing fear. *Run*, I think to myself, the short, dark hallway preventing escape.

"Jackie." The tone of his voice asserts his power over me. I must resign myself to what is to come. I, we, have been here before.

I do not run. I do not fight. No one else is home. Besides, he is my big brother. He is the boy. He is *the* boy. I am just a girl who needs to be seen and not heard. There is nothing I can do to protect myself.

LIE NUMBER THREE: ANGER IS VIOLENCE

The horror of having someone disregard my "no" in such a profound way decimated the power of my words. When left with the ability to say nothing, the only other option for protest becomes physical. If I can't **say** no, I can **demonstrate** my no. If I cannot argue with or against you, I can push you, hit you, show you my protest through anger.

Try and silence me, and I'll come unhinged. Disregard me or diminish what I'm trying to say, and I'll come unhinged. How many times did my sweet husband walk into the minefield of abuse triggers without knowing it? How many times did it happen without me knowing it? Surviving abuse left me with little awareness of its impact. The slightest increase in volume or tone of voice left me panicked, and my go-to defense was explosive anger. Without healthy boundaries or reasonable communication skills, I was a hot mess.

PERFORMANCE *anxiety*

❧☙☙☙❧

I have learned Post Traumatic Stress Disorder is real and has a name and a life all its own. I have learned it is a sneaky bastard who holds you hostage. PTSD is the holder of silent Stockholm Syndrome—the condition where misplaced, irrational feelings of trust, affection, or sympathy are felt by the abused toward their abuser. You don't see it coming. You don't know it's there until somebody tells you. And then the hurt you hate and would never wish on another becomes your reality. Your handiwork.

I feel like my heart is full of love and gentleness and other-people goodness. When I look out from me, I envision extending my arms in an embrace of "It's okay." Or at least that's what I thought. This was my image of me. Maybe, as I turn to you in a critical moment, my heart is full of one thing, but my arms are holding a flame thrower. Maybe instead of turning to you in love, I turn and douse you with flames without even knowing it. PTSD has blinded me.

I'm sorry. I didn't know. I am full of this goodness, and I didn't know I was holding the freaking flame thrower. I didn't know I was hurting you.

❧☙☙☙❧

I didn't know there were words or actions (outside of abuse) that would impact me so directly, so immensely, and overwhelmingly. However hard I tried to be heard, however desperately I wanted and needed to be heard, my porcupine-studded volatility made it very difficult for anyone to endure listening. The less I felt heard, the stronger my reaction. All the time, I just wanted to be heard. I just wanted someone to understand me. My thoughts. My opinions. Just choose me. And I acted in ways that made that all but impossible.

Even when faced with a "normal" disagreement with a "safe" person, as a sexual abuse survivor, I often resorted to physical violence rather than try to voice my thoughts through dialogue. This was especially noticeable when the other person in the disagreement was adept at verbal argument. Knowing I had no voice, I seldom mustered the courage to try and express myself verbally, fearing I'd only be shot down or outwitted by a better debater. I often responded by striking out physically. I may not have continued the cycle of sexual abuse, but there's an almost certain chance I perpetuated the cycle of abuse in another form.

LIE NUMBER FOUR: I MUST PERFORM WELL TO BE ACCEPTED AND LOVED

You remember that I had an adopted brother and sister. Or at least I did. Not anymore. By now I was an only child. At least that's the story we tell.

෴ೞೞೞ෴

It had been about a year since we moved back to Michigan to live near our family again. Mom came into my bedroom, "She's run away again," her worry and frustration were obvious. "Did you see her leave?" she all but whispered.

I pause. *She's run away again?* They've never asked me before. I didn't know she'd done this before. I'm certain Dori would not want me to tell the truth, but the hurt in my mom's eyes prevents me from doing anything but.

"Yes," I gulp, "She crawled out the window."

PERFORMANCE *anxiety*

Dori and I share a bedroom on the lower floor of our split-level duplex. It was easy for her to step up on the table between our beds, open the window and hop out.

"It's a full moon tonight. She must have planned it so she'd be able to see …" my dad talks to my mom as if I weren't there. "Did she say anything?" he almost pleads with me.

"No," I wonder how much to tell, "she didn't say anything. She just looked back at me, and I pretended to be asleep." *She's run away again. How many times is again? How many times has she done this?!*

I am somewhat aware of Dori being in trouble. A lot. She is always screaming at my mom. There is a lot of slamming doors and loud sighs and arguing. And there was that one time I overheard my parents' tense conversation after she'd done something wrong.

"This has to be punished," mom insists. "She cannot get away with this again and again …"

"Come with me," dad demands of Dori as he walks down the hall to her room.

I wonder what he plans to do. *What consequences will she get this time?* I sit in the kitchen, trying to avoid being noticed. If Dori sees me, if she knows I'm aware of her being in trouble, it will certainly mean something bad. She's good at taking her frustration out on me.

After what seems like only moments, Dori storms past. Her face is red with rage, but she is not crying. She is angrier than I've ever seen her. She yanks the front door open with purpose and slams it behind her.

Dad follows her, but he stops in the hallway between the front door and the kitchen. He glances toward the door Dori just slammed. His face is troubled. He looks weary. His eyes turn to my mom, and they share a look of sadness between them. Neither says a word.

∽∾ଔଔଔ∽∾

Years later, I would learn about that day. The breaking point of that day. In one last attempt to corral 6+ years of lies, theft, fighting, and what today would be characterized as oppositional-defiant behavior, my father took a belt to Dori's backside. The shame she had brought upon our family was met, finally, with the intensity of her burden. Within months, she was pregnant. Seventeen. A junior in high school. She and the father were married shortly thereafter, set up in an apartment, and both families rallied around these two lost teens who would become parents at an all-too-young age. It wasn't long after she gave birth that Dori split with the baby's father and cut off all contact with our family. Was it easy to let her go? I don't know. What I do know is we never saw Dori or her little girl again.

∽∾ଔଔଔ∽∾

Unlike Dori, quite the opposite, in fact, John was an all but perfect son. He had the family name. He had the family looks. He had the family smarts and athletic prowess. John never gave anyone any trouble. John was a straight-A student and a starting player on the high school soccer team. As a junior, he received an athletic scholarship to Wabash College. We were all so very proud of him. *Of the golden child. The heir.*

"What do you mean he's rolled his Jeep down the hill? Is everyone alright?!" My dad's voice pleaded for everything to be alright. Dad drove an ambulance when he and mom were first married. He'd seen the impact of roll-over accidents …

"One of the girls is hurt pretty bad … her leg … hospital … sue …" Dad's face grew more and more concerned.

※☙☙☙☙☙※

"He's obviously sneaking out the back door when we've all gone to sleep," they discussed. "We just can't trust him anymore."

※☙☙☙☙☙※

"I found these under his bed," mom gritted her teeth. "He's bringing drugs into our house now! He's bringing it here!!!"

John's footsteps thundered up the stairs from his basement bedroom.

"You had no right!" he screamed, "No right at all! It's my room! It's mine!"

"No," dad countered, "it's not your room. It's my room. In my house."

"Screw you!" John's words punched my parents, "Screw you and all your rules!"

※☙☙☙☙☙※

"I'm sorry, Mr. Wiersma," the Wabash College representative spoke with regret, "I'm really quite sorry, but John's failing all but one class … Just not the kind of candidate we hope to have … Going to have to rescind the scholarship offer …"

The words broke his heart. The shame of his son's failure slammed full force into his chest. How could he tell his father, his very proud, very demanding father, that John would almost surely fail out of high school, that he'd lost his scholarship and his future?

❧ ଓଔଓ ❦

I found the book on the kitchen counter. "What's *Tough Love*?" I wondered out loud to an empty room.

The voices in the other room let me know John and my parents were having a very serious conversation. Muffled sobs were met with angry words I couldn't quite make out.

"I'm sorry it's come to this," my father all but cried, "but you can't make the choices you are making and stay in this house. We have Jackie to think about. You simply cannot drink and do drugs and fail out of school and stay here. You'll have to find somewhere else to live."

I was naïve to John's drinking and drugs. The abuse I suffered at his hands had ceased when I started my period (thank God). My interactions with him were few and far between, thanks to school and sports. Although I knew he did things that angered my parents, I didn't realize why the minister was visiting a lot or why we saw John less and less on the weekends.

❧ ଓଔଓ ❦

Then just like that, John was gone. My parents had done an excellent job of shielding me from the very real struggles of parenting an addict. One day John was there; the next, he wasn't. Over the years, extended family whispered about John's absence and the choice my parents had made in protecting me and forcing John from our home. Had they done the right thing, kicking him out? What kind of parents do that? Couldn't something more have been done to help John?

Just as it had with Dori, John's behavior had brought untold shame and hardship on our family, and he was no longer welcome. I knew in a very real way that not doing the right thing or bringing shame on the family had consequences. You could and would be disowned.

∽ఊఊఊ∽

I know how to be seen. I am a pro at appearing happy, being polite, helpful. I can avoid trouble at any cost. I know how to be a good representative of the family at all times, in all places. I would never embarrass or bring shame on the family. I know which fork to use at a formal dinner and how to sit still in church. My clothes are chosen for me, down to the dress I wear for my high school senior portrait. I know how to be seen. And not heard. I am a pro at performing these and any number of tasks my family may ask of me. I do what is expected, and I am accepted. I am loved. This ingrained philosophy is what led me to sports. Because performance brings acceptance, and it makes my family proud when I win.

In order to be the good child, the acceptable child, I found swimming. Swimming was my meditation. The pool deck was my altar. The bright spot in a very dark and shame-filled home.

LIE NUMBER FIVE: IF I PERFORM TOO WELL, I WILL BE HATED

I've always been driven. It's how we roll in my family. Performance is key. It never occurred to me to do less than what was expected. The blessing is that doing my best produced notable results. The curse is that doing my best produced notable results. Results that got me the love and praise of my family and coaches often brought the criticism and condemnation of my peers. The better I performed, the more my family lavished me. The better I performed, the more my peers bullied me.

As I attempted to find my place, misunderstood patterns from an untold and hidden abusive childhood found their way to the forefront. The sexual abuse I had suffered at the hands of my adopted brother and his friends had taught me my value was in my sexuality. Preteen wonderings led to a "boyfriend" on the swim team. While I swam laps, lost in the slow lane, I found the positive attention I craved on the back of the bus. We had kissing contests with another pair of swimmers. I honestly had no sense what I was doing was wrong, let alone embarrassing or shameful. I knew firsthand sexuality equaled value and love, and I was basking in every moment of that affirmation.

> *I honestly had no sense what I was doing was wrong, let alone embarrassing or shameful.*

Swimming had, more often than not, been my place. My space. The only location where abuse could not touch me. Unfortunately, high school upended all that. The team initiation had always been to choose one freshman and, as a team, induct her by giving her a swirly. Fun stuff. The absolute terror of having your teammates grab you, carry you—kicking and screaming—to the toilets, and then turning you upside-down into a toilet bowl and flushing it feels as fresh today as it did 36 years ago. The sting of knowing you were the one worthless person an entire team chose to indoctrinate added significantly to my feelings of worthlessness.

PERSONAL *anxiety*

Despite the shame of the swirly, I stayed on the high school swim team. As a parent myself, I cannot for the life of me understand how bullying and hazing played such an accepted role in athletics when I was a preteen and throughout my teen years. Perhaps it was part of an unaware social structure, or maybe it was partly the result of abuse that taught me to "put up and shut up." Either way, I knew then that I had no voice, was not valued, and needed to keep quiet about all of it.

Nicknames abound from freshman year. Spaz. Flatsy Patsy. Wierdsma, to name just a few. Again, I found myself in a place where I just didn't fit. All the moves had robbed me of the familiarity and relationship, however unbalanced, of growing up with peers over time. No one knew me, and I didn't know their accepted routines or conversation, or games. I was an easy target. At 13, I was a young freshman. I swam in the slow lane reserved for those who made the team, but were not fast enough to win races. I wasn't valuable.

Fast forward to my junior year … I was swimming well. I was now valuable to the team. Or so I thought. An unprecedented turn of events found me receiving that freshman swirly again. The more I improved in the pool, the worse treatment I received from my teammates. The van ride home from an away meet left me with a wad of gum in my hair. The physical traits and energy that made me a good swimmer also made me a good joke.

I learned that I wanted to be vanilla. Not too much. Not too little. Blend in. Avoiding notice was safe.

Our 200 freestyle relay team broke the record. That was good. Being the anchor for that was good. Our 200 medley relay team broke another record. That was good. Being the anchor on a second record-breaking relay was good. Breaking the record for the 50 free was good. Breaking the record for *my event* was good. Breaking the record for the 100 free was good. Breaking the record for *my* second event was good.

"I'm putting you in the 100 back today," my high school coach, Scott, directed.

"But I don't swim backstroke?" I questioned.

"Let's see what you can do," he offered.

"Okay then."

I don't understand. And I hate backstroke. You have to get into the cold water before you even begin the race. But, whatever. Scott says I'm swimming backstroke, so I'm swimming backstroke.

Swimming this event means I'm in the lineup at a different time than usual. I'm on edge, worried I'll miss my event. Routine is reassuring. I know how to succeed in that routine. This change, however seemingly small, makes me feel unsure, almost out of control.

As the 100 back approaches, I anxiously walk over to the starting blocks. *I don't want to get in the cold water.* I realize I can maneuver myself around the starting block and stand on the gutter to position myself for the start of the race. I don't have to get in beforehand after all.

Phew. Nice.

"Swimmers, take your marks," the official announces.

I crouch into starting position. Adrenalin pushing through me. Muscles tensed and waiting to be released.

Bang! The starting gun reverberates throughout the natatorium.

I push my legs as hard as I can and arch into an unfamiliar backstroke start. My body streamlines underwater, and I kick fiercely until I surface midway down the length of the pool. I suck in the chlorine-filled air and pull, one arm after another, until I reach the wall. I tuck into a ball, coaxing my 6' tall frame into the smallest space possible. I turn, push off the wall and repeat my effort for four lengths of the pool. I am unaware of anything but the movement and effort of my body and the water. The shouts from my coaches. Scott wants me to swim this event. I will swim it. *I. Will. Perform.* I arch my back, stretching for the touch pad, aware only of finishing and looking to the time clock to see how I've done. I look up. Scott is jumping up and down; a huge smile turned my way. I look up to the stands, not understanding my coach's excitement. The parents in the stands are cheering, sharing hugs and high-fives. I look back to my coach, still not grasping why everyone is so excited.

"You broke the record!" he shouts.

"What?" I am confused.

"You broke the record!" he shouts again.

It takes a moment for me to realize what he's saying. I smile. Unbelieving. And then I join in the celebration. I smile back. Big. And I look to the stands and smile—big—before exiting the pool and returning to my teammates. Girls, jumping up and down and shouting, encircle me. I am elated. I have done well, and everyone is happy with me … with my performance.

This scenario repeats itself often that year. New events. New records. I feel more and more valuable. I begin to gain some confidence that I really can be appreciated and accepted. I really am worthy …

"She can't swim the 100 fly," they argue, "It's not her event. It's not fair. That's Brittany's event! Jackie has every other record on the board, and she doesn't need Brittany's. It is just not fair!" Brittany's parents argue with the coach.

THE LIES SHE BELIEVED

Their glares turn to me. An undercurrent of tension ripples through the team. I am met with sideways glances. Brittany has her friends on the team. They gather around her. I'm not sure why, but the teammates I thought liked me, accepted me, now distance themselves. It is clear I am the problem.

"We're changing the lineup," Scott shares.

"Okay?" I question. I am not arguing. I am perplexed.

"Brittany'll be swimming the 100 fly. I'm moving you back to the 100 free." He looks almost defeated.

"Oh. Okay." I run through the order of events in my mind. I'm not sure why there is a change, but I'll do whatever my coach asks, understand or not. Maybe doing what he wants will show my teammates I am part of the team. Maybe swimming "my event" will make room for someone else. Maybe if I just do what I'm supposed to do and "stay in my lane," they'll like me again.

What I do know is that I've crossed a line somewhere. By just being me. By doing what my coach has asked of me, I have become the enemy. *I take it back*, I think to myself. *I take back the records. I take back being better. I just want to fit in. I just want them to like me. I take it all back.*

I swim the 100 free. I do well. I win the event for the team.

"Good job," the assistant coach beams.

"Thanks," I reply sheepishly. *Please don't let them think I'm too happy*, I think, looking toward my teammates.

Scott gives me a hug as I walk back to the side of the pool and the gaggle of screaming excited girls. I barely smile at him. *I won't make too much of my success.*

PERFORMANCE *anxiety*

A few girls offer high-fives and congratulations. I smile, but not a big smile. *I am not too good. I have only made a small contribution.*

My goal, my performance, switches from doing the best I can and relishing the praise and acceptance to doing my best but shrinking from the praise or celebration that might threaten others. I will do my best—my God-given best—but I will not hurt anyone or anger anyone else, lest I be a problem.

I am comfortable being less than.

I want to be invisible.

Invisible is safe.

ENDNOTE

1. https://www.scientificamerican.com/article/infant-touch/.

chapter four

PATTERNS

We're fickle, stupid beings with poor memories and a great gift for self-destruction.

PLUTARCH

"How could you do that to me?! Cole growled. "How could you possibly embarrass me in front of my friends? I can't believe you did that!" he slurred through a drunken rage.

Cole was my boyfriend. We met in the Quad at a freshman mixer. He was the antithesis of my "type." He was just my height, so too short. Red-headed. Not a traditional boy, he had a bit of edginess about him. Instead of being a textbook athlete, he was a cheerleader. He was strong. He could pick me up and toss me around with ease. He was quiet and didn't draw too much attention to himself. All this taken together made him interesting to me. My attraction to him felt bold, a chance for something different. He was a total gentleman and sweet to me. After my experiences with John, it felt really nice to be liked and have someone enjoy my company without pushing for more.

PERFORMANCE *anxiety*

I felt safe with him. I liked that he liked me, so when I embarrassed him, and he got angry, the shame was overwhelming. I, a Division 1 swimmer, had double false-started. I had disqualified myself, lost points for my team, and apparently, brought unequaled shame upon my boyfriend. His words hit stronger than any fist ever could. As an athlete, my body knew punishment. I could physically endure unfathomable pain. But this, this assault on who I was and how horribly I had performed for him, broke me.

The lessons of an entire childhood came into stark relief at that moment. I had learned early, and well, that performance equaled acceptance and love. The usurping of my place in my family had long been overcome by performing as the "good girl." I did things right. I did things well. I danced the dance 24/7 and relished the approval I so often mistook for love. Never would I do anything to bring the kind of shame my family felt from John and Dori. Never would I put myself in a position where I might be disowned. Never.

Not only would I stay away from lying and cheating and stealing, I would stay away from alcohol and drugs. I would not yell. I would not fail. Not in school, not in sports. Not in anything. I would prove I was worth loving. I would be perfect in everything. I would show them they had chosen poorly in those other two. And perform I did.

The moment I opened my eyes to such total disappointment in my performance changed how I saw things. I had a glimpse that performance could not only make me, it could break me. The boyfriend who, just moments before, held all my hopes and dreams and positive affirmations turned on me like a viper. The sting was unbearable. I would spend the better part of two years trying to reconcile how I could adore someone so very much and allow an equal but opposing hurt into my heart.

PATTERNS

The pool was no longer my safe zone. I wasn't the fastest on the team as I had been in high school. I didn't have a solid grasp on what it meant to be a scholarshipped athlete. I kept on performing, but my performance was riddled with insecurities and no father figure to provide constant affirmation.

Just as my swimming faltered, so did my academic performance. I, like many others, had not needed to nor learned how to study effectively in high school. The challenge of college classes added more insecurity to my already faltering drive. The more I struggled, the more my anxiety to perform grew.

I was a good student in high school. I naively believed I could and would rise to the challenge of the business classes my initial college major required. I was, of course, enrolled as a business major. Because I was now the only child, I was the only option available to take over the family business. It was what my dad wanted, so it was what I did.

All too quickly, I found myself failing calculus and barely passing several other introduction-to-business classes. I had to weigh the obvious disappointment of failing classes and not living up to expectations with pursuing something I loved.

I had absolutely no idea what degree I wanted to pursue. As I flipped through the course catalog, I recalled the consistent praise I'd received for my writing throughout middle school and high school. I had garnered approval there, so I thought that was what I should pursue. Certainly, I'd succeed in writing where I failed so abysmally in business. I boldly changed my major to Creative Writing, aching for the success that would bring acceptance and admiration.

PERFORMANCE *anxiety*

I began the second semester of my freshman year with a sense of relief and possibility. This semester would be different. This semester would be better. My hopefulness was extremely short-lived.

"If you've chosen writing as your major," Professor Young announced in front of the Creative Writing 101 class, "I strongly encourage you to reconsider." My cheeks flushed under the heat of public humiliation. Even my chosen major was a place of condemnation. My choices were not enough. I was not enough. Instead of finding like-minded peers and encouraging professors, I found disapproval. I just wasn't performing well enough—again.

The cycle of internal struggle played out once more. I tried to do what was expected of me. I failed. I tried to do what I wanted. I failed. I retreated to doing what was expected. If I couldn't succeed at one, I'd succeed at the other. I had to succeed at something. Failure was simply not an option.

> *The cycle of internal struggle played out once more*

On to college major number three.

I loved to read. After two years of high school Latin and another two years of high school Spanish, I was confident with foreign languages. Changing my major to English Literature with a possible minor in Spanish seemed a logical choice. The first semester of my sophomore year, I dove into classes I thoroughly enjoyed. I felt more secure in my academic performance as my grades rose. The security of good grades, however, didn't make up for the scrutiny of my peers. I enjoyed Spanish but was often mocked for being the "class nerd." I thoroughly enjoyed English Literature and decoding the beauty of *Beowulf* in Middle English but was met with equal disdain from my classmates. It became obvious what I liked was not where I would find acceptance from my peers. I'd have to find something else to study.

As I flipped through the course catalog, I recalled my "What I Want to Be When I Grow Up" paper from elementary school. *When I grow up, I want to be a teacher.* So, for the fourth time, I changed my major. This time to Education. That was until I shared my choice with my parents.

"You can't be an education major," my father directed. "You'll never make enough money."

Well, alrighty then. I stank at business. My professor shamed me out of creative writing. My classmates laughed me out of English Literature and Spanish, and my father had just negated Education as a major. The clock was ticking. I had a significant number of classes completed but no direction. I sorted through all the credits I'd accumulated and settled on Professional Writing—major change number five.

The perfectionist in me loved the professional writing classes. I thrived as the consummate proofreader. I liked catching mistakes. I would get my degree and be done in four years. *I have to do this in four years.* I had that box to check.

I was on to the next class. The next degree. The next whatever it was that I could perform.

∽ ෬ ෬ ෬ ∽

In an attempt to find solace from Cole's criticism of my swimming and the rebuke of academic peers and professors, I continued seeking the attention I would so often mistake for love. My father's joking words pointed me in a very focused direction. I would get my "Mrs. Degree." After all, I always did what my father told me to do, directly or indirectly.

PERFORMANCE *anxiety*

I wanted, more than anything, to make things right with Cole. However, I couldn't get past knowing I'd disappointed him. Obviously, I needed to keep looking for Mr. Right. My father had told me I'd find him, after all. So, full of determination and refocused effort, I looked for someone more like my father, someone who would fulfill every dream I knew my father and mother had for me.

There was that one guy …

His dark hair and light eyes had caught my attention more than once that fall. Just like Cole, he wasn't as tall as the guys I'd swam with and dated in high school, but his dark Scotch-Irish good looks and noticeable well-built physique stood out. Although we lived in different dorms, being in the same freshman quad and eating in the same dining hall offered plenty of opportunities to see one another. I wrestled with my feelings for Cole and the physical attraction I felt for someone else, but Cole had made it clear—I was a disappointment—and I let attraction override feelings. Feelings didn't matter anyway. I had to find Mr. Right.

My roommate, Kris, and I walked toward the dining hall. After two-a-day practices, food was high on our priority list.

"So, how was it in the distance lanes today?" I asked.

"Long," Kris laughed. "You have it so much easier as a sprinter."

I laughed.

"When the going gets tough …" I began.

"The sprinters get out," she finished.

We both joked.

"Hi," he interrupted.

"Oh. Hi," I smiled.

PATTERNS

Kris and I paused.

"You go ahead," I encouraged. "I'll catch up with you in a sec."

Kris continued to the dining hall, and I stood, giddy bubbles in my stomach and a huge lump in my throat.

"I'm Chad," he said. I could feel the heat from his body.

"Jackie," I smiled.

"So, I was wondering," he smiled back, "if you'd like to go out sometime?"

School girl giggles filled my head. He was so handsome. And built.

"Umm. Sure. That'd be great," I smiled back.

Chad. His name was Chad. And he wanted to go out with me. *Me.* I was ecstatic. I all but ran to the dining hall to find Kris and my other teammates. He wanted to go out with me ... I couldn't stop the cyclone of thoughts whirling through my head. What if ... So cute ... Maybe ... I wonder ... Oh, please, oh please, let him be the one.

Our first date was to the Mexican restaurant uptown. The details of getting there and back, what we ate, what we said are a blur. Saying goodnight, however, not so much.

We ended the night on the front steps of my dorm.

"Thank you," I smiled. I couldn't stop smiling. "That was nice."

His smile and light eyes focused intently on my face, my mouth. As he leaned in to kiss me, I put my hands on his chest.

"I've been thinking about that for a long time," I whispered afterward.

"Oh, really?" he grinned.

"Yeah."

"Well, how about we go out again?" he proposed.

"I'd like that." My smile gave away any sense of reason or respectability.

"Good," he grinned.

Several weeks later, I found myself in his dorm room. Young college co-eds, my drive to find Mr. Right, and the lessons of sexual abuse pushed me forward to the only place I understood love to exist.

"But I can't offer you that kind of commitment," Chad shared in the midst of fumbled intimacy.

"That's okay," I all but pleaded. *This must be right. This feels right.* I didn't need him to promise forever … yet. I just needed him to love me …

John had shown me what love looked like, or so my wrongly twisted self thought. And now John was out of the picture. My college life was getting underway, and the hope of my future seemed bright. I thought I was free. I had Chad, and he loved me—tonight had proved that—and I would make everything all right again. I could fix it.

≼ଔଔଔ≼

Chad began his second semester by pledging a fraternity. I was excited for him and looked forward to the fun he, and we, would have. I wasn't allowed to join a sorority; my parents believed it would unfairly divide my time between swimming and Greek life. Shortly after Chad completed his fraternity "hell week," there was a large party to celebrate.

"What do you mean you didn't get the invitation? The pledges went to all the sororities and personally handed them out?" Chad asked angrily, resentfully. *How could I be so stupid? Of course, I wouldn't get one. I'm not in a sorority.*

"Apparently, they left yours at the bell desk. You were the only one not in a sorority." His disdain grabbed me through the phone.

"You need to find it to get into the party!"

I rushed from my room to the lobby desk on the first floor of my dorm. No one sat there, and my pulse began to race as I frantically searched for where my invitation might be. *It must be here!* I flung desk drawers open in desperation. *It must be here!*

I opened the last drawer and found it filled with pens and random sticky notes. There, under all the clutter, was my invitation. "I'm not in a sorority," Chad's words echoed back to me. *How will I ever do this right?* I picked up the invitation and went back to my room, both relieved and defeated.

⋘ ଔଔଔ ⋙

Weeks passed filled with class and practice and fraternity obligations. It felt as if Chad and I didn't have enough time together. I was thrilled to learn of a team party and couldn't wait for us to go together.

"There's a swim team party this Friday. Do you want to go with me?" I asked.

"No. They're not really *my* people." Chad dismissed the opportunity. "How about you and I just hang out, the two of us?"

Chad never came to my meets. He never wanted to hang out with my teammates. *Silly me. What was I thinking?*

As a male, Chad's approval was tied to my dad's approval and was a stronger pull than the approval of my coach or team. My performance mattered, but my connection—a source of comfort, acceptance, and affirmation, took a back seat. These were not Chad's people, so they could no longer be my people. Chad did not approve of them. So, without knowing or understanding why, I began to pull away emotionally from the very people with whom I had found belonging.

I wanted, needed, was almost desperate to secure my relationship with Chad and, indirectly, my father. If something wasn't acceptable to Chad, it wasn't acceptable to me. His likes and dislikes informed mine. Little by little, without even realizing it, I withdrew from anything and everyone outside of Chad. I was an isolated island of one, and he was my only lifeboat.

⋙ ⋘ ⋙ ⋘ ⋙

"Susan has some new things for us to look at," my father shared, "I thought we could go over Saturday, and you could try everything on and see what works."

"Sure," I capitulated. I tried not to sigh too loud, but I dreaded the experience.

This is what we do. This is what we've always done. My father chooses my clothes. He has for as long as I can remember. Every season Susan, the manager of the women's department at my father's favorite store, sets aside tops and pants and skirts and sweaters she thinks we will like. Dad and I venture over and I, like a trained seal, try on all the new things, modeling them before dad chooses what he thinks looks best. Fitted, structured outfits. No frills. No girly colors or fabrics. I was *stylish*. I always look good, at least according to my father.

I will never forget when I discovered the Laura Ashley store at the mall. The florals. The colors. The flowing, feminine designs. Everything about the store sang to me. Everything about the store was the direct opposite of the clothes I wore.

I knew I'd never be allowed to buy such frilly things, but I yearned for them, nonetheless. In an attempt to avoid disappointing anyone and somewhat choose for myself, I begged my mother to make me a few dresses based on the Laura Ashley dresses I adored.

"Mom, please?" I smiled my biggest smile. "You can sew so well, and the pattern looks really easy and pleeeeease???"

"Oh, alright. I'd be happy to," she smiled back at me.

I wasn't defying my father. I was just stretching my wings …

Mom and I went to Jo-Ann Fabrics and selected the pattern and fabrics for our sewing project. It felt invigorating and daring. It was enjoyable, just us girls, choosing girly things.

"What do you think?" I asked as I twirled in the beautiful, new jumper my mom had fashioned just for me.

"It's… Well… There isn't much shape to it, is there?" my dad offered.

"I know, but isn't it pretty? Didn't mom do such a great job? Don't you just love it?" I offered as much positivity as I could muster. He *had* to agree.

"Yes, she did a lovely job," he answered.

More than anything, I heard what he didn't say. He didn't say he liked it. He didn't say it was pretty. He didn't say I looked pretty. What I heard him say and not say all rolled up together was that I hadn't chosen something good enough. My choices were not good enough. I wasn't good enough.

My choices were not good enough. I was not good enough.

PERFORMANCE *anxiety*

A couple of years later, when I'd observed and cataloged the various outfits popular around campus, I tried my hand at fashion once more. I pulled out a crisp, white t-shirt and a heavily starched, ankle-length chambray skirt. As I looked at myself in the narrow dorm mirror, I knew the outfit needed something more.

"*A belt. This needs a belt,*" I said to myself.

I pulled a red belt from the closet, and my red slip-on flats catch my eye.

"*Those will coordinate nicely,*" I confirm.

I finish dressing, grab my book bag, and head out the door for class. I am confident in what I'm wearing. I think it is the most beautiful, well-coordinated outfit. I walk across campus, a smile on my face. And person after person I pass looks me up and down and… snickers. They assessed my outfit and openly laughed.

I chose. I felt good. I got snickered out.

I guess I didn't know anything about fashion. I never had the opportunity to learn it. When I tried, I failed. No one had approved. I'm really not good enough. So, I reverted back to the wardrobe my dad picked because at least he was happy.

⊷ ෴෴෴ ⊶

Every time I felt any safety or security, my true self tried to emerge. She wanted out. Desperately. But every time she surfaced, someone played whack-a-mole with her and put her back underground, stinging from the backlash. Every time I tried to just be me, I quickly learned I was, in fact, not enough. I had to abandon myself. My confidence crashed, only reinforcing that I needed to move on to the next thing—the next boy, the next class, the next major, the next choice.

PATTERNS

I thought I could perform my way to love. Again and again, no matter how hard I tried, it became abundantly apparent that I couldn't. Still, I could not shake the pattern. Performance was my only avenue to acceptance—I would just have to try harder.

PERFORMANCE *anxiety*

I thought I could perform my way to love. Again and again, no matter how hard I tried, I could not.

chapter five

NATIONALS

For a minute there, I lost myself ...
LYRIC FROM KARMA POLICE

Seeing him was like being t-boned by a freight train I never saw coming.

It had been four years since he and I were in the same room. Four years since my parents had kicked him out. Four years free from his torment, free from abuse. I was finally at a place where I felt like I came first—even if I wasn't a boy, at least I was a great athlete. At last, I was free from John.

But there he was, standing between mom and dad on the balcony of the Indiana University Natatorium. Maybe it was one final attempt between a sober John and my parents to make amends, I don't know. But when I saw him, I froze. *What was he doing there? Why had he come? Why was he with them? What did this mean?* I froze, my thoughts jumbling together in rapid succession, each one more horrid than the last. I was terrified. Confused. Utterly lost. His presence was my rejection. In my mind, no other explanation was possible. Choosing him was not choosing me.

Thousands of spectators, swimmers, coaches, and judges were present. Their conversation settled into a loud roar, and distinct voices are hard to pick out. Just as if I were in a movie, everything in my head went silent. It was as if every other thing in the room was blurred out and drowned out, but the sight of John standing between my parents and the sound of my own blood rushing through my veins pounding in my ears.

I fell in line behind my teammates. I dove into the icy water and followed the person in front of me through the warm-up.

Between the warm-up and the competition is a blur. I know I got out of the pool. I know I dried off and got dressed. I know my coach, teammates, and I went out to dinner and made our way back for the big event, but I cannot recall a single detail.

I went on autopilot, returning for the qualifying round. Our relay team was seeded near the middle of the pool as one of the faster teams for that heat. Behind the starting blocks, the faces of my teammates were familiar but not comforting. I joined in, jumping up and down, shaking my arms, and trying to loosen up and get ready for the race.

I should be feeling something right now. Adrenalin should be informing my brain to kick in the endorphins needed to speed through the water, but all I felt was numb.

"Swimmers to the blocks," the announcement came. Sue stepped up on the block, with the rest of us falling in behind. *She is going to lead us to victory because that's what we do. We are Miami University's swim team, and we win championships.*

NATIONALS

"Swimmers, take your marks," reverberates as the loud crack of the starter pistol startles me and momentarily shakes me from my angst. Sue enters the water, and we rush around the starting block to cheer for her. Kathy steps on the block, ready to go in as the second leg of the relay.

I looked over at the clock. 22 seconds. 23 seconds … and Kathy is in the water. We help Sue out and resume cheering for Kathy. I start to feel the pressure. Meg is the third leg, our fastest swimmer; then it will be up to me—the anchor.

We are doing well. In the blink of an eye, it's my turn. I get up on the starting block, my eyes follow Meg down the pool and back, and I keep waiting to feel "it." The feeling I get when I win. I don't think about it, ever; I just feel it. But I don't feel it, and I have a lightning-fast 22 seconds before Meg touches the wall, and I reach out my hands and propel myself into the pool.

I am in the water, but I forget how to swim. My body knows what to do, but I can't remember how. Muscle memory by definition. *I can't feel the water.* After training and tapering and shaving, I can't feel the water. Every swimmer can feel the water. Not that day. Not me. It was like swimming through pudding. Nothing made sense. When I surfaced after the flip turn, I was disoriented. I wasn't where I should have been in the rank of things. People were ahead of me when they should have been next to or behind. When I touch the wall, I don't need to look up at a time clock or my teammates. I know I've blown it. *Things can't feel that wrong and turn out alright. I couldn't have failed that badly.*

But there you have it. I stood next to my teammates on the pool deck. No comments. No looking around. I had failed. I failed my teammates. My school. I'd failed my parents. My family. I'd failed

PERFORMANCE *anxiety*

"Coach." I'd failed every person that had ever done anything to help me as a swimmer. And I knew it.

This failure felt like something from which I would never recover. Like the marker between B.C. and A.D., there would be life before Nationals and after. Nothing would ever be the same. The pool would remain, in some way, my safe place. The pool is where I had escaped John's abuse, and because Chad never ever came to the pool for any reason, the pool is where I also escaped from him. But because I had failed so badly, I didn't think I could stay in the pool anymore. Such was the level of my toxic performance theology. Acceptance was my god, and performance was my rite of worship. Failure was blasphemy, and banishment was the punishment deserved for my sin of failing.

∽ଓଓଓ∽

I gathered a strength of self I didn't recognize. I would be brave this time. I would be honest (or at least as honest as I felt safe being). I would tell them …

I adored my "Little Peanut Grammie." She, barely 5 feet tall, was so tiny next to my 6-foot frame. She was generous. She had a wicked sense of humor. She was the matriarch of the family.

I was excited to be having lunch, just us girls. Time away from school. Swimming. Chad. The sun radiated through the atrium glass. What was once a Wendy's restaurant was now a lovely soup and salad spot for ladies to lunch. The ice in the water glasses sparkled. The music hummed something pleasant in the background.

"Good afternoon, ladies," the waitress welcomed us.

"Good afternoon," my Mom and I responded in unison.

NATIONALS

"Can I get you something to drink while you're looking at the menus?" she inquired.

"I'd like a coffee," Grammie began.

"And I'll have a diet Coke," Mom said.

"Coke, please," I added.

"Perfect. I'll be right back. I can answer any questions you have about the menu then," the waitress smiled and went for our drinks.

Now. Do it now, before she comes back, I all but pleaded with myself.

∽ ☙❧❧ ∽

I'd lived with my absolute failure at Nationals for months. I had put my heart and soul into swimming up until then. It had never been about how fast I could kick or how strong I could pull. As long as I knew who I was and for what I was valued, I swam. The moment my heart was no longer in it, swimming ceased for me. My talent was as strong as ever. My speed was as fast as ever. But I no longer cared about swimming. It was no longer a safe haven for me. When he showed up on that day, at that meet, I gave up.

I had wrestled internally with quitting since Nationals. I didn't discuss it with my coaches or my team. For perhaps the first time in my life, I considered something contrary to what I knew was expected of me. I contemplated walking away from the very thing that brought my acceptance, adoration, love. *How the heck was I going to tell my family?*

∽ ☙❧❧ ∽

"Mom. Grammie. I've been thinking … I'm not sure I want to swim anymore."

PERFORMANCE *anxiety*

Blank stares met my words. The proverbial pregnant pause. I fought down regret. *Why had I said anything? How stupid could I be? What was I thinking?! Did I expect them to support me? Did I …?*

"You have a gift from God, and if you do not use it, I will disown you," my sweet Grammie countered.

Of course. How silly of me. There is one right way. And that is my way. And that is God's way. What an ungrateful child. God had given me a gift, and I wasn't going to use it? I wanted to retract my words. I wanted to erase every single thought I'd ever had about quitting swimming. I was such a horrible, ungrateful person not to use the gifts God had given me. I had used my voice and found out that it was blasphemous.

This was me looking for my voice. It took an enormous amount of courage to drum up the nerve to speak to them about stopping something they wanted for me, but I did not want for myself.

> *It took an enormous amount of courage to drum up the nerve to speak to them …*

In that instant, I learned that it is not safe to share the intimate, in-most parts of me with the people who love me. This restaurant meeting informed the lie if I am fully known, I will not be fully loved. So, I need to hide the parts of me that are disagreeable or maverick or unlovely because if I let these out, I am not lovable. If I let these out, they will know I am small. Ugly. Afraid. No, it is better if I bury those things deep. Maybe they will go away, or maybe I will just better learn how to pretend. For sure, I won't say them out loud again. I do not want to be disowned like John or Dori. I want to belong.

NATIONALS

I sought a fair hearing. I risked trust. I hoped for understanding and empathy. I longed for comfort and acceptance. Instead, I was met with a disappointment so deep I would not understand the wound until many years had passed and many layers of life had covered over this brief moment of raw exposure.

I walked away from that lunch with an even more in-depth understanding of family expectations. I would push through. All the doubts I had would have to find somewhere deep within to hide. The only truth I needed to understand was God's truth, my family's truth.

I'm sure neither my mom nor my grandma had any idea of the weight of this moment or how indelibly it would be etched into my soul. They knew I was good at swimming and likely just wanted to encourage me and not see me give up on something. They didn't have the insight to see that my request had little to do with the pool and everything to do with the abyss I was in. They didn't know they were resigning me to accept abuse silently and compliantly. Had they known, I'm sure the conversation would have looked much different. But as a family, emotional intelligence was not something we had ever known to develop. Intuition to look deeper and go beyond the surface was not something in which we were skilled. So, this chat that they may not even remember marked a dark turning point for me.

Why was I making things so complicated? Besides, the pool was my place to escape *him*.

Oh. They didn't know about him, did they?

PERFORMANCE *anxiety*

chapter six

ESCAPE

... these are the boundaries ... an intoxicated yes is still a no.

HENRY MCCORD, HUSBAND/FATHER, *MADAME SECRETARY*

I never felt I could have an opinion of my own. I thought I had to perform to expectations to be loved and accepted, and that sex equaled love. I thought I had to come out of college with an engagement ring on my hand. I would do whatever it took to meet my family's expectations. My experiences at the hands of John without the protection or intervention of those who loved me left the stain of abuse on my soul. And like a wolf picks up the scent of its prey, the smell of abuse clung to me. It was on the wind through every flirtation, no matter how innocent. Having been abused, I was the perfect candidate to seek out the familiar, twisted comfort found in an abusive relationship.

The twisted dance of abuse sows outcomes much like the survivors of the notable bank robbery in 1973 Stockholm, Sweden. After being held hostage for six days, the captives went on, to everyone's shock and dismay, to advocate for and even raise money to defend their captors. At some point in those six days, aggressor became friend. Friend became ally. And all those who worked tirelessly to protect and rescue the captives became the enemy. This phenomenon of a victim bonding with their abuser became known as "Stockholm Syndrome."

If there is just enough truth to the lies, they are believable. If there is just enough kindness alongside the abuse, it is tolerable. If there is just enough … You get the idea. And somewhere in the process of feeling trapped in abusive situation after abusive situation, the abuse victim can develop an unhealthy perspective about the situation and the people involved—about themselves and their abusers. Up becomes down. Right becomes left. Wrong becomes right.

What do you do when you meet "Mr. Right?" What would you be willing to endure if you knew Mr. Right was exactly what your family wanted for you? How would you perform to keep Mr. Right, just so you would know your family would be pleased with you, and as a result, love you? I stayed in this abusive relationship because I didn't feel worthy or that leaving was an option. This wasn't a literal restraint, and in my case, not even an economic one. I firmly believed this was my best opportunity for love and acceptance—both from him and my family. This perception closed off the option to leave. For me, that option simply did not exist.

No had never worked out for me, so I didn't know I could say no. I had no concept of what it looked like to establish a healthy boundary or hold myself in high enough esteem to consider I had any right or responsibility for my mental, emotional, and physical well-being. It never crossed my mind. I had met "Mr. Right," and if sex was the best proof I had that he loved me, how much more loved could I be than to have this man wanting me anywhere and everywhere he could? He must love me. He must *really* love me.

It wasn't so much that I didn't want to say no. Believe me when I say that there was a little girl screaming no at the top of her lungs inside me. There was a little girl full of shame wishing she could run away and never look back. That little girl also knew she was not allowed to say anything lest she cause trouble like John and Dori. Lest using her voice resulted in being cut off, disowned. It was 100% understood that I was to marry *this* man. I knew I was expected to perform perfectly for the primary male in my life. Until now, that had been my father and performing for him looked like being seen and not heard, doing what I was told without complaint or question, keeping up appearances, so my behavior never cast a bad reflection on the family's honor, and being the best at what I did. With this new man, my perception of performance was informed by my childhood roles of demure duty. With this man, performance meant keeping quiet and enduring whatever he asked of me and did to me to earn and keep his approval. That is what good girls did. Good girls, Wiersma girls, didn't rock the boat.

> ...performance meant keeping quiet and enduring whatever he asked of me and did to me...

Fraternity parties and bars with friends meant alcohol, so at least there was the numbing effect of drinking whatever beverage was put in front of me. Burying your head in alcohol is one thing; burying your heart in the fog of drunkenness isn't quite as effective.

Swimming was a great escape. Alcohol was an even greater escape. The longer I stayed with Chad, the more frequent the abuse occurred, and the more I drank it away.

PERFORMANCE *anxiety*

◈✿◈✿◈

"Good morning," Chad spoke softly to wake me.

"Good morning," I smiled, my head thick from a night of bar-hopping. I rolled toward him, curled up under the many blankets on the daybed in his mother's guest room.

He climbed into bed next to me, and I was glad for his snuggly warmth.

"How are you this morning?" his kisses gently encouraged me awake.

"Mmm … I'm good now," I offered as I returned his affection.

Gentle kisses quickly became more intense, his intentions obvious.

"What about your mom?" I cautioned.

"We'll just have to be quiet," he winked.

"Are you sure? Really?"

"Yeah. But keep quiet. She'd kill me if she found out."

That didn't stop him.

◈✿◈✿◈

Does the inability to say no mean that I was to blame? At what point does reasonable intimacy between two adults become abuse? Is it all okay, no matter how degrading or selfish, unless the girl has the courage to give a verbal "no"? Do men bear any responsibility for pushing and manipulating, and grooming their victims? Psychological abuse almost always accompanies sexual abuse, and the societal nod of "boys will be boys" often paints them as dashing rogues, while the women upon which they prey are labeled as fast, loose, and promiscuous. Nothing could have been further from the truth.

◈ ೀ ೀ ೀ ◈

"Follow me," Chad took my hand.

"What?" I struggled to understand him over the blaring music.

He grabbed my hand. "Come on."

His mischievous smile both enticed and frightened me.

"Where are we going?" I all but yelled.

"You'll see …" he slurred.

We made our way from the makeshift hot tub in the fraternity's front yard to the great room inside. I guzzled more of my drink as he led me through the throng of co-eds dancing and drinking. The crowded room gave way to a just-as-crowded hallway. Chad turned the corner toward the bedrooms.

I was surprised when, instead of continuing on to his room, he pulled me into the group bathroom. *What the heck*? I wondered. Surprise quickly turned to fear as I followed him, stumbling drunk, into the group showers. *Are we rinsing off after being in the hot tub*?

Chad wrapped his arms around me as he turned on the water.

"Ooh! That's cold!" I shivered.

"I can fix that," he grinned as he pulled me to him and under the water. Before my intoxicated mind could register what was happening, he had my bathing suit off.

"No!" I screamed, terrified. "Stop!" I pushed him away from me, and he stumbled backward.

PERFORMANCE *anxiety*

He regained his footing and glared with the ferocity of a wild animal, "Fuck you!"

I wrapped my arms around my naked body as he all but ran out of the showers. Several of his fraternity brothers turned back to look at me. My eyes fell to the floor, shame forcing me back into the darkest recesses of the showers.

"Can you get me a towel?" I called out, desperate. "Please. Can someone get me a towel?"

After what seemed like an eternity, someone tossed a towel to me. I wrapped my dripping wet body as best I could and made my way to Chad's room. His roommates and their dates filled the small space.

"Can you help me find clothes? Something? Anything?" I pleaded.

"Chad's drawers are over there," one of the guys pointed, "I'm sure you can figure it out yourself." The disgust in his voice deepened the self-loathing I already felt.

I tried to open drawers, searching for a shirt, shorts, anything to cover my nakedness and shame. They were all locked. One of the guys finally threw a bunch of clothes at me. I managed to pull out a pair of cut-off sweatpants and a t-shirt and dashed out the door into the hallway.

"Have you seen Chad?" I called out to a familiar face.

"Yeah. He's passed out in the front yard."

Really?! Seriously?! What an ass! I'm done! Really and truly done!

My bare feet crossed the front yard without seeing him as I ran and stumbled the half-mile to my dorm room across campus in the freezing November cold.

ESCAPE

It was one of the first times I said, "I'm outta here," I went to my former roommate to talk about what was happening and ask for help. She listened and validated my need to leave. I called Chad to end it with her sitting next to me; her presence and witness were an overwhelming emotional support. Within 15 minutes, I was walking to his room.

She was absolutely disgusted and disappointed. "How could you? Why would you?"

I did not know how to express my anxiety that I had just broken off "the" relationship that was meant to be my "happily ever after." In the back of my mind, I heard my father's voice, "You're going to get your Mrs. degree." I had tried using my voice before with a dreadful result. This was my father's expectation of me, and I needed—make that I was driven—to check this box. The crumbling picture of daddy's little girl walking down the aisle with the beaming pride of parents and guests had the force of an electromagnet to a small steel ball. I couldn't disappoint them all like that. I had a twisted idea of what covenantal marriage and traditional roles meant. *"Mr. Right" is my ticket. He is going to do everything for me. He will make it all better. He will take care of me. No one else will want me. If I leave, I can't do anything for myself.* The anxiety turned to panic, and I rushed to his room, terrified Chad might not take me back.

Like many women under the spell of an abuser, I felt deep shame and guilt. I felt responsible. I felt like I had to stay no matter what. I suffered from Stockholm Syndrome. I had these weird, misplaced feelings of trust and affection for my abuser. The thought of having no connection was far more frightening than this twisted,

I felt like I had to stay no matter what.

dysfunctional connection. I had made this bed; now I had to lie in it. It was time for me to suck it up, bury my feelings, and get on with it. The reality that my parents had disowned John and Dori—John having once been the golden child around whom such affection, admiration, and family pride had been placed—terrified me. If they could erase John from the family portrait, then I could be erased too. I could not let that happen.

He took me back. I hadn't blown it. There was still hope for me. An injury kept me out of the pool, my safe (and healthiest) escape, so the destructive pattern of our relationship continued: class, alcohol, a flesh-hungry fiancé … but at least I was engaged. That had to count. That made the behavior acceptable. It was all going to be okay.

Until it wasn't …

It was not until winter training of my sophomore year that a believable opportunity to leave the pool presented itself. During dry land training, while pressing 180 pounds, the most intense, searing pain possible ripped through my left ribcage. I re-racked the weights and stepped to the side, and tried to breathe through the pain. The team finished up the weight training portion for the day and headed to the pool. Diving into the water brought the sharp, searing pain back. I tried to swim through it, but as I reached my hands over my head to streamline off the flip-turn, I could barely breathe.

I dropped down underneath the lane lines and half-doggie-paddled to the side of the pool. I called out to get my coach's attention.

"What's wrong?" he asked.

"I don't know," I struggled, "but it hurts really bad right here, and I can't breathe."

"Well, Jackie, hop out of the pool, sit out for a bit, and rest and see if it gets to feeling any better."

ESCAPE

There was no assistant coach, so his focus was on running practice. I inched to the handicapped steps and gingerly made my way out of the pool but sitting out brought no improvement.

I was not given to pain. I was not one to ever get out of the pool or quit or pause, so before long, Dave recognized there might be something that needed attention, and he took me to the Emergency Room.

He stayed with me through triage and nearby during the initial examination. The pain was no better, so they gave me medication and ordered x-rays. When it looked like it would be a while before there would be an answer, he let them and me know that he needed to get back to practice and oversee all the other girls. I could sense his uneasiness and appreciate that he was responsible for a whole team, not just me.

They wheeled me back to radiology, and the blissful fog of the narcotics had really taken the edge off the pain. I relaxed a bit. It seemed like only a short time before my coach had returned.

"Hey, Dave," I greeted him as he came into the room.

"Hi, Jackie," he answered.

"So, what did they say? Am I gonna live?" I joked.

"Well, nothing's broken," he began, "so I suggest we head back, and we'll see how practice goes tomorrow before we make any decisions."

We returned to the Hansel and Gretel Inn, where I slept off the effects of the pain medicine, and the next day, I tried to get in the pool again.

The pain returned, just as bad as before, so Dave offered that I just do kick drills and not raise my arms above my head in the water.

PERFORMANCE *anxiety*

My teammates lapped me again and again as I puttered through the water. All I could think was, *I don't belong here. I don't want to be here anymore.*

I got out of the pool, went over to Dave, and said, "This just hurts too much." Pushing through was no longer on my mind. I didn't care. I wanted out.

After practice, we telephoned my parents, who were staying with my grandparents just a few hours north, and they came and got me. I spent the rest of the week on pain medication and muscle relaxants, resting in my grandparent's guest bedroom.

The day before the team was ready to drive back to Ohio, my parents drove me back down to meet them. I was waiting for my teammates at the hotel when they came back from practice.

"I didn't think we would ever see you again," one of them said. Her words solidified my belief I didn't belong in the pool with these enormously successful athletes anymore.

Somehow, I managed to endure the long ride back to my school with the team. The next day, I saw the university's physical trainer, who concurred that there was likely significant soft-tissue damage. The trainers put together a plan to allow me to do some modified dry land training while I recuperated. Watching my teammates practice while I did dry land training didn't motivate me. It only further widened the gap I felt between us.

I never got in the pool again. I was driven out not by injury or pain but by the long shadow cast by failing at Nationals. The rest of the team had quickly moved on, but I had never recovered from losing the race for my team.

ESCAPE

~ ❦❧❦ ~

Spring Break was meant to be the perfect opportunity to lift my spirits after such a difficult winter. Chad and I boarded the plane for Florida and some much-anticipated time with my parents. Sun. Fun. Food. Family. We would figure out how to fit us all in their 40-foot motorcoach, but I couldn't imagine anything more wonderful than spending time together—my perfect guy, the beautiful pearl and diamond ring on my hand, and my parents. What could possibly go wrong?

"Welcome to Florida!" my mom beamed as Chad and I exited the jetway.

"Hi, Mom," I walked into open arms.

"Hi Chad," my father extended his hand for a firm handshake.

"Hello," Chad smiled.

"Glad you're here," my dad gathered me into a gentle yet strong hug.

"Hi, Dad," my smile grew even larger. *We're here! This is going to be great!* I thought to myself.

The heat and humidity of Florida winter washed over us in stark contrast to the Ohio winter.

"Phew!" I panted. "It's hot here."

"Welcome to Florida," my mother chuckled.

The drive to the RV resort passed quickly as we made light conversation.

The look on Chad's face changed as we pulled into the parking space in front of the RV. I wasn't sure why, but he looked upset.

"Everything okay," I asked.

PERFORMANCE *anxiety*

"Yeah, sure," came the unconvincing reply.

"Well, here we are," my dad presented his pride and joy, "40 feet of mobile luxury. Better than any hotel."

"Two TVs, a VCR, a microwave …" I was both proud of and embarrassed by his description.

Mom opened the door. "Let's bring your bags in, get you settled, and then we can relax with something cool to drink."

"Sounds good," I agreed as I climbed the few steps inside.

"So, we have the master in the back. One of you can sleep on the sofa here in the main area, and the other will have to sleep on the floor."

I looked over to Chad and hesitated.

"Jackie can sleep on the floor," he stated matter-of-factly, as if an order.

"Oh … well, okay," my mom didn't argue with him, but the look of disappointment and dissatisfaction on her face told me exactly what she thought of him taking the bed and leaving me with the floor.

∽଼ଓଓଓ∽

Despite what I knew to be a rocky beginning, I did my best to make sure everyone was happy. Mom and I laughed and joked and cooked while my dad and Chad "bonded" over beers. Chad and I went to the RV Resort water park and went alone to walk on the beach and play in the ocean. Dinners out were another opportunity for fun.

"Cheers," my dad lifted his glass.

"Cheers," we echoed back.

ESCAPE

"So, what's everybody having for dinner?" my mom inquired.

"I'm getting the death dog!" I answered. Duffy's death burger and death dog were the spiciest things on the menu. Layers of hot sauce and jalapenos and horseradish assaulted your tastebuds, and dad and I had a tradition of eating one with enough beer to wash it down.

"Death burger for me," dad agreed.

"What about you?" I looked to Chad.

"Not for me. I'll just have a hamburger."

Bummer. I thought to myself. *Would be nice if he'd join us.* I immediately began thinking of what I could say to make him feel more included. I wasn't sure why, but I knew it wasn't okay for Chad to choose differently. My dad didn't say anything, but Chad's irritation was obvious.

Our final day in Florida felt strained. I secretly wanted to stay with my parents and avoid returning to school with the man I knew I had to marry but was very quickly learning to dislike. My mom and I went inside to pack up and leave my dad and Chad to talk, just the guys.

A short time later, Chad flung open the door.

"Can we go for a walk?" he insisted.

"Sure," I replied, wide eyes looking to my mom and then back to him.

No sooner were we outside and down the short driveway and Chad unleashed.

"Your dad doesn't really like me, does he?" Chad accused.

"Of course, he does," I encouraged, "What would make you think that?"

PERFORMANCE *anxiety*

"I mean, he just told me he's going to sell all his companies and retire." Chad's utter dismay shocked me.

"What? What do you mean?"

"Your dad just told me he plans to sell everything!" he shouted. "Everything!"

I didn't know what to say. *Dad said what? Why?* The plan had always been that Chad would take over the company.

"You knew, didn't you? You must have known!"

Confusion and panic overwhelmed me. I knew nothing.

"I'm just as surprised as you are."

"Right! Sure! You've always known he didn't really like me, and now this! I have to go call my dad."

As Chad walked away, I felt my world growing very, very small.

∾☙☙☙∾

Many years later, my father would share with me his perception that Chad was with me, for the most part, because of the opportunity to take over his company. (He had no idea the many other physical reasons Chad and I were together.) In an epic stand, my father took the very thing he thought Chad wanted away, trusting the rest to God. Neither of my parents had ever really liked Chad but didn't want to interfere directly. They had decided they'd let things "play out" until our visit with them in Florida.

Chad's behavior and the apparent dis-ease of our relationship compelled my father to take action, however surreptitious. Taking the proverbial carrot away seemed an insightful and logical thing to do.

ESCAPE

Chad would either prove my father wrong and stay with me regardless, or he would show his true colors and leave.

I did everything I could to ensure he didn't. An already tumultuous relationship only became more so. Chad's need for physical satisfaction and connection increased as the security of his professional future became uncertain.

I had used the pool to escape my abuse from John. I had escaped from the pool when it was no longer a safe haven for me, and I turned to Chad. I both wanted to and was terrified by the thought of escaping Chad. But escape had become my thing …

PERFORMANCE *anxiety*

*Don't judge yourself by
what others did to you.*

C. KENNEDY, ÓMORPHI

chapter seven

IT ALL COMES CRASHING DOWN

In order to rise from its own ashes, the phoenix first must burn.

OCTAVIA E. BUTLER

The day finally came. Summer break and separation. I was nervous and unsure. Would the relationship last long distance? If there was no opportunity for sex, would Chad's love for me diminish? I was desperate for the summer to go by and for school to start again.

Unlike the previous summer, there were no trips back and forth to see one another. I took a job working full-time modeling at our local department store, and my bruised, thirsty ego basked in the praise I received there for my height, athletic build, and attractiveness. Chad never praised my appearance. He made me feel guilty for being taller than him, so I often slouched and always wore low-heeled shoes when I was with him. I craved the security of his attention. Phone calls left me feeling disconnected and anxious.

PERFORMANCE *anxiety*

I needed the reassurance that my connection to him protected my future. I needed his desire to prove I was desirable.

At long last, summer drew to a close, and we packed up my things to leave home and go back to Miami University in Oxford, Ohio. I was both anxious and eager to return. The opportunity of a new year, new classes, and Chad made the 5-hour drive from Michigan seem like 10. My father sped through the rolling hills and farmland of rural Ohio. As we crested one last hill, Oxford came into sight. I felt more at home than I had all summer. Rental trucks and cars pulling trailers crowded the streets. Parents and students carried boxes and beds, lamps, and suitcases into houses and dorms and apartments. My anxiety gave way to excitement. I was here. He was here. It would all be okay.

We circled the block several times before we found a place to park. No longer part of the swim team, I was left to my own devices to haul my gear up three flights of stairs to my dorm room. A moment's hesitation and the effort of it all reminded me that I'd lost my safe space and teammates to help carry the load. I quickly pushed the sadness and disappointment aside and smiled an expected smile as my dad and I passed each other in the hallway. I had, after all, chosen this. I was excited, I told myself. I. Was. Excited.

Thirty minutes after unloading the first box, we closed the trailer door. Dad and I spoke nervously, trying to find the words to say goodbye.

"Well, I guess that's it," Dad offered.

"Yes. I guess so." I shifted my feet and looked around.

"Thanks for all your help."

"You're welcome. Happy to do it," he replied.

IT ALL COMES CRASHING DOWN

I stretched out my arms as I closed the space between us. "I'm going to miss you."

"You'll be okay. And we'll see you soon," he promised as he held me tight.

"I know," I whispered through my tears.

Why? Why was I crying? So silly of me. This much emotion just wasn't necessary.

"Well, I guess you should go. You still have a long drive home."

"I do," Dad brushed away a tear that had dripped down my cheek. "Be good. And if you can't be good …"

"Be careful," I filled in the quote he'd shared with me every year since I'd gone to college. "Love you."

"Yep. Love you too," he smiled as he got into the car.

I waved half-heartedly as he drove away. My focus turned quickly and completely on getting my room set up and, most importantly, seeing Chad.

∽ ଓ ଓ ଓ ∽

My heart palpitates. My adrenalin is coursing with nervous anxiety and anticipation. I finally get to see *him*. I walk from my dorm toward the fraternity house as he walks from his fraternity house toward me. I am eager to look into his eyes, curious what I will find. Maybe it will be better now. We made it through summer break and were still a couple. The nagging fears of not being enough, of losing him and my future settled a bit. My pace quickened; I approached him, giddy and full of smiles.

He hugged me, but something was different. Wooden. Distant.

He took a step back, ending our embrace. Troubled, I looked into his face. It was flat. Emotionless. No desire. No hunger. No sign of regret.

"I don't want to be married," he said. It was matter of fact, like, "I don't want chocolate cake."

In complete disbelief, all I could do was say, "Oh, okay."

He turned and walked away.

Blindsided and numb, I stood there for a moment, speechless, unable to will my feet to take a step from that spot. My autonomic nervous system took over, and I walked back to my dorm. I climbed the three flights to my room, and in utter defeat, I began unpacking. "I have absolutely no future," I whispered.

•~°03°03°03~•

I am alone. Utterly and truly alone. The realization came crashing down around me. All the cards of all the choices I'd either made or been coerced into making for the past year and a half came crashing down around me.

At least if I hadn't quit swimming, I'd still have those friends. If I'd gone to see him this summer, maybe he wouldn't have left me. If only …. Thoughts of confused desperation plagued me.

"You can't wear heels," Chad instructed. "I don't like it when you're taller than me."

"You know those jeans look good on you, don't you," Chad all but sneered at me, "You want all my fraternity brothers to ogle you, ***don't you?***" Jealousy oozed out of him like an infected sore.

IT ALL COMES CRASHING DOWN

∽ಲಿಲಿಲಿ∾

"Don't," I screamed as I pulled my swimsuit top back into place.

"What's the big deal?" Chad laughed at me and to all the other people in the hot tub. "Nobody saw anything anyway."

∽ಲಿಲಿಲಿ∾

"That dress looks nice on you," he smiled. "but …"

I tuned out the rest of his words. I often heard compliments taken back with a tell-tale "but" after them. I knew anything good he would say came with a "but." I didn't often measure up.

Every negative comment and perceived criticism came flooding back as I tried to decipher what I could have done differently. Better. *If only I'd done better, he would have stayed.*

∽ಲಿಲಿಲಿ∾

"By using isolation as a method to cut a dating partner off from family and friends, the partner who is using abusive behaviors has a greater amount of control in the relationship. Isolation can also create the space in a relationship for the partner using abusive behaviors to escalate other harmful behaviors.

Ultimately, the survivor may feel like they have no one to talk to about the abuse they are experiencing, leaving a dating partner without a support system during their greatest time of need."[1]

Abusive partners isolate their victims from family and friends to increase their control over them.

PERFORMANCE *anxiety*

☙ ༄ ༄ ༄ ❧

"Wiersma," Chad called up to my open third-floor dorm window. "Wiersma," he called again. And again. Wasn't this the man who had begun our junior year by telling me he didn't want to be married? Not married, apparently, but friends with benefits, you might say. He called up to me. His call was insistent. His call wouldn't cease until I came down and let him in.

He loved me, after all.

All that sex … wasn't that proof that he must somehow still love me? Maybe, just maybe, he would change his mind. He was, after all, the man I was supposed to marry. He was the man who was supposed to take over my dad's business. Me loving him wasn't a requirement. I just needed to regain his acceptance. I needed him to step back into the plan. Utterly confused and conflicted, knowing I was being used but unwilling to face that reality, I answered Chad's dorm window calls week after week after month after month. Each time, feeling more and more soiled. More and more trapped. More and more desperate. Used and discarded, I grew more and more ashamed.

☙ ༄ ༄ ༄ ❧

James Taylor played on my boom box; his deep, moody melodies and lyrics were a tonic. I sat on my bed, and Laura stood leaning against the desk. We had swum together our freshman year and reconnected. We talked about everything and nothing, sometimes lapsing into easy periods of silence, just hanging out. She was ivory snow clean. Pure. She knew where she was going and what she was doing and had a confidence and grace about her I admired. She was everything I was not, and I marveled that we were friends. I didn't feel worthy of her friendship, but ever so grateful we were.

I was about to turn twenty-one, and Laura and I were making plans for my celebratory pub crawl and who we wanted to go along with us when the too familiar voice of Chad bellowed from below, "Wiersma!"

Like a child caught with their hand in the cookie jar, I froze. *Does she know?* I wondered. I hoped she didn't. I didn't want anyone to know about these hook-ups. I was no longer the only girl on Chad's hit list, just one of the charter members. Shame enveloped me.

Laura looked at me (it felt like through me) and said, "What the heck is that about?" She looked confused and irritated that someone would be so rude.

Oh God, just let him stop; I shuddered. I did not want to tell her what was going on, not wanting to lose her acceptance. I looked at the blanket, unable to meet her gaze, and said, "It's Chad."

"Wiersma!" he called again, demanding an answer.

The look on her face told me that her disgust was with him, not me. She studied my face, questioning, and I got the nerve to say, "He won't stop unless I let him in."

"What? Why?" she asked, incredulous.

"This is what he does. He drinks with his friends or goes out on dates with girls who won't give him what he wants, and then ends his nights by coming to me," I answered in defeat. I couldn't believe I said it out loud. It was like the first time I admitted how awful his behavior was and how low I felt for being *this* to him, for him.

I looked up at her, feeling desperate and hopeless, "He won't leave me alone," I almost whispered. "He always finds me …"

PERFORMANCE *anxiety*

In true Laura form, matter of factly, she said, "THAT is not okay, Jackie. That is just NOT okay."

"But … he always finds me …" I repeated, "He always finds me …"

"Okay then. You come and stay with me," she was stepping in to intervene. There was no way she was going to let Chad find me in her room.

In that moment, I felt like I could breathe for the first time in a really long time. I did not feel condemned. She didn't make me feel stupid. She just offered help. Offered hope.

My dear friend, Laura, stepped in in an active intervention for my physical safety. When I didn't have the strength to pull myself out of the lies and torment of abuse, she took me to a safe space, bubble-wrapped me for a season, and gave me the foothold to walk away.

I went with her to her dorm room and slept on her floor. I slept better than I had since returning to school. I slept in safety.

Chad never came back to my room again.

ENDNOTE

1. https://www.breakthecycle.org/blog/know-signs-spotlight-isolation-friends-and-family.

chapter eight

TURN THE PAGE

To be fully seen by somebody, and be loved anyhow—this is a human offering that can border on miraculous.

ELIZABETH GILBERT

Laura never left my side. Nights and weekends, we were studying or hanging out together, or she was just a phone call away. I never went anywhere alone. Laura had a great network of friends, and they welcomed me into the fold. This was a great posse of people to play quarters with, bar hop, and just enjoy being young. In this group were several nice-looking young men who were fun to flirt with, and when they flirted back, it made me feel worthwhile and attractive. After Chad, my esteem was shattered, so I craved this attention more than ever.

For me, flirtation was an invitation, and that invitation meant I would be loved.

We had been drinking and playing games at Laura's house.

PERFORMANCE *anxiety*

We all walked uptown together, stumbling and bumping along the sidewalk, already under the influence. We picked C.J.'s as our destination. The smell of beer and body odor met us long before we walked inside. The floor was slick and sticky. The lights were low, but not low enough not to see the filth, just dim enough to hide.

Laura sees some guys she knows at the bar. She smiles and waves, and they motion for her to come over. I know none of them, but I follow Laura. I go where she goes. As we walk across the floor, the guy with bright blue eyes and dark hair catches my eye, and I catch his. The chemistry was instant and intense. A round of introductions was made, but the smoldering eye contact between us continues. Before long, we are no longer part of the group; we pull aside and just talk to each other. He looks at me, "You want to get out of here?"

"Yeah," I say.

He grabs my hand, and as I turn to walk out behind him, I look at Laura and say, "See ya' later!"

This was not the first time this scenario unfolded, and it would not be the last time. What I knew was that I would be loved. Accepted. Valued. Whatever you want to call it, in my mind, this is what sex was. It was proof I was lovable. Proof I was desirable. Proof I would not end up alone.

❧☙☧☙❧

Girls who are sexually abused when they are young end up with a very mixed-up idea of love, life, truth, value, and worth. Something evil wraps around their core memories that teaches them sex = love. Their value is equated with a physical demonstration of acceptance or approval—and not the healthy kind. Most do not know how to communicate about their abuse as it is often a close friend or family member involved, and they have not yet developed abstract thinking or the language they need to say what is being done to them or by whom. They often feel guilt and shame, and their abusers often feed into their fear of being discovered or of telling anyone about any of it.

Abuse victims long for connection, and as those little girls turn into young women, many grow up to embrace abusive partner after abusive partner. They often use sex as a means of gaining some sort of control. It is rarely ever about the sex. It is about fulfilling a need to be loved. The pattern is vicious and ugly. It does terrible damage that, without intervention and a path to healing and restoration, will mar and scar the victim for life.

I was this girl. I did not know what a healthy male/female relationship looked like. Yes, I had a father who loved me and never once did an inappropriate thing to me. But he was not a demonstrably affectionate man. He didn't give out lots of hugs or kisses on the forehead. I did not witness my parents holding hands or cuddling. I think I just put him in a totally different category altogether. I knew I was expected to marry, and I believed the only way I would find a man who would marry me was if he loved me. And the only way to prove he loved me was to have sex with me. It was a twisted, ego-crushing, psychologically destructive pattern that continued through the rest of my junior year of college all the way through my senior year until … I met Brigham. Again.

During my freshman year at Miami University, there was this really cute naval aviator and Resident Assistant. Although he was attractive, I was already distracted elsewhere. As I walked out of the dorm where he was an R.A. one day, he said, "So, when are we going to go out?"

PERFORMANCE *anxiety*

He was not as tall as the 6'5" guys I usually dated, so I answered, "I'll go out with you when you grow a few inches."

And we both moved on.

We had no interaction between that awkward freshman encounter and the latter part of my senior year. *Top Gun* was *the* movie, and I had seen this guy around campus who had dark hair and wore a leather flight jacket. He had all the appeal of Tom Cruise on the big screen, and I was instantly attracted.

After another fun night of drinking games at Laura's, our crew made our way back uptown. I went upstairs at one of our favorite bars to use the bathroom, and when I came out from the back, I saw "the guy." Dark hair. Leather flight jacket. *There he is!* I thought.

Full of liquid courage, I walked through the crowd and made my way over to where he stood. I tapped him on the shoulder, and he turned around. But it was totally not the guy I thought it was.

It was Brigham.

Wide-eyed, I choked out, "Brigham??"

We had not spoken in years, and at that moment, I did not remember that I said he was too short. There, face-to-face, he was handsome. *Really* handsome. A quick conversation led to, "So, do you want to get out of here?"

"Yeah," I smiled.

And the next day, he made me dinner.

And the day after that, we jumped into his sexy RX-7, and he drove me to Cincinnati for a dinner date.

We saw each other every day for two solid weeks, then I caught the flu and got really sick. I was sleeping on the couch in my apartment, so I wouldn't get my roommate sick. I felt miserable, but Brigham brought me chicken soup and popsicles, and medicine. He slept on the floor beside the couch where I lay. Protective. Concerned. Kind.

I had never had anyone really take care of me like that. Really take care of me.

I thought to myself, *I could marry this guy.*

And I did.

⊰ ☙☙☙ ⊱

Brigham's gentle attention and kind affection felt beautiful and terrifying all at the same time. It felt like what I thought love should feel like, but it was not the kind of love I had yet experienced. I kept waiting for the other shoe to drop. For the fairytale to end. For Brigham to grow tired of me or discover the ugly parts of me and walk out the door. I had no concept that a person could be fully known and fully loved. I just knew this man was different, and I wanted to spend the rest of my life with him.

⊰ ☙☙☙ ⊱

We both knew the other had a past, but we never talked about it. We never asked each other about past relationships, and I found it comforting to pretend that my past was different than it actually had been. The longer we were together, the easier it got for me to rationalize away that part of my life—to rewrite that version of my childhood and adolescence and superimpose a different version on top of the real one, suppressing the anguish and anxiety, the guilt and shame.

PERFORMANCE *anxiety*

With Brigham, I turned the page and began a new chapter. I did my best to place an iron lock on the early pages of my diary, throw away the key, and never flip through those pages again.

I believed if I could just perform well enough and be a good enough wife, a good enough mother, that maybe, just maybe, he wouldn't leave. I could play this role, and I got pretty good at it, but I walked on pins and needles every day. I had this nagging fear in the back of my mind that I might not be good enough. I might slip up and say or do something displeasing and spoil it all. Ghosts never leave you, even if they mostly wait until you are alone before they return to haunt you.

> *Ghosts never leave you, even if they mostly wait until you are alone before they return to haunt you.*

Despite everything I tried to be and do, the impact of years of abuse left me with a volatile and aggressive temper. I didn't know how to fight fair, and every argument left me petrified that Brigham would leave me. In true victim mentality, after any fight, I quickly went back to grovel, believing that if I were the first to apologize and take all the blame and all the responsibility for what had happened, he might be compassionate enough to stay. To give me another chance. To not leave me.

Hard as I tried for this new chapter to have nothing spoiling it from the last one, the old fears and destructive patterns of thinking began surfacing between the lines.

chapter nine

SURFACING

Today, I am working on improvement, not perfection.

JACKIE MCCOWN

About six years into our marriage, Brigham and I both knew something needed to change and sought out Christian counsel. With one meeting, it became abundantly clear I had things that needed to be worked through. But those "some things" still didn't have a name. I still had not said these things out loud to another human soul. I had never shared the story of what had happened to me with anyone, and I was not about to do it now.

We met with our counselor, Larry, together and also separately. For reasons I do not understand, at my next meeting without Brigham, I spilled my guts. Larry strongly encouraged me to share my story with Brigham.

The next joint session, I sat down on the couch, knees together, hands clenched, a lump in my throat.

"Hi guys," Larry began our time together.

"Hi," I replied, a little too brightly.

"Hello," Brigham offered as he joined me on the sofa.

"Well, I think we should begin today with where Jackie and I left off last time, if that's still okay with you, Jackie?"

"Umm. Yeah. Sure."

"Okay then. How about we pray, and then you can start?"

"Sounds like a plan."

Larry led the three of us in prayer. His words barely registered; my mind fully focused on telling Brigham about John and Dori. *Will he understand? Will he hate me? Will he think I'm dirty and ugly and want to leave?*

"… Amen." We lifted our heads, and my eyes made their way to Larry for reassurance, security. I shifted my glance to Brigham. *Please, God, don't let him leave me.*

"So, you remember my adopted brother and sister?" I began.

"Yes?" Brigham questioned, not the memory of them but as an encouragement to continue.

"Well …" I held my breath, turning to look at Larry once more. *Please, God, give me the words.*

"Well … They weren't always nice to me." Inhale. Exhale. Breathe. "Actually, they were mostly not nice to me."

"Okay?" Brigham's gentle eyes waited for me to continue.

"They would hurt me. Do mean things." I stopped and started. Paused in fear, wanting to go on, but terrified my brokenness would be too much for Brigham to stay. My heart raced.

"Can you tell me what?" he asked.

"Well …" my words echoed the depth of my torment and fear. "They did lots of things."

"Can you give an example?" Larry gently prodded.

Inhale. Exhale.

"They would do this thing … They would put me head-first in a sleeping bag and then push me down the basement stairs, and I would crash into the fireplace hearth at the bottom."

Inhale. Exhale.

"And then they'd just leave me there."

I looked at Brigham. His eyes were sad, caring.

"And they'd chase me around the house and grab me and hang me upside down over the upstairs railing."

"I'm sorry," Brigham shared. "I'm so, so sorry."

"Yeah. Thanks." I didn't know how to receive the love he was giving. I'd never told anyone, and no one had ever shown me compassion as he was in this moment.

"Wow …"

"Yeah. I know. Right?"

"I'm so sorry they did that to you," Brigham repeated.

"They weren't nice."

"No. No, they weren't," he agreed.

"Part of the things Jackie and I have been talking about is how their actions impacted and continue to impact how she deals with conflict ..." Larry's words faded off into mumbling. I've opened the door to John and Dori, but I've managed to keep the deepest, darkest ugliness hidden. *Maybe I can tell part of the truth, and things will be okay. Maybe Brigham won't leave. I can do this.*

But I stopped there. I didn't tell him about the other stuff. It was too humiliating. It was locked away too deeply. This piece of the truth was enough to explain my issues. *God, let it be enough.*

※☙☙☙☙☙

It would be another 12 years before we openly discussed John and Dori again. There were children to raise and careers to advance. Counseling. Learning. Changing. Growing. All the while, God was working quietly behind the scenes, preparing me to trust another with my truth. Preparing me to be loved.

"Hey Mac," I offered one day with the most lighthearted voice I could muster.

"Yes?"

"I was wondering if we could talk?"

"Sure?"

Trepidation filled the space between us. "Can we talk?" is usually not a good thing. "Can we talk?" usually leads to more-than-difficult conversations. Arguments.

"It's okay," I offer. "I just want to share something with you."

"Okay …" his voice trailed off, perplexed, anticipating possible unpleasantness. "Where and when would you like to talk?"

"I was thinking my prayer room? If you had time today?"

"I can do that. Can you give me 10 minutes, and I can be ready?"

"Yes. I can do that," I confirm, smiling just enough to try and convince him, or myself, things are all good, that this conversation isn't anything too difficult or too challenging.

A lifetime of anxiety and performing rush forward. My hand tightens around the railing as I climb the stairs to my prayer room.

It's going to be okay. God has brought you to this place. Mac loves you. You are not just the brokenness of your past.

I—we—are finally at a place in our relationship with God and each other where telling my whole ugly, tarnished truth can happen. I finally understand that stay or go; I need to be completely honest at this time with this man. I closed the door and settled into the corner of the love seat. I have sat here many times—in prayer, in tears, in laughter. This is *my* safe space. This is the place I have ministered to others, and God has ministered to me. The light from the floor-to-ceiling windows was bright and hopeful. The pinks and teal blues of the furniture and décor were soft and gentle. The words painted across the wall behind me remind me of a never-ending truth.

"In quiet and trust is your strength." – Isaiah 30:15

I wait. Anxious and at peace. Emotions battling one another, fear trying to prevent me from bringing the truth to light. I breathe in the stillness I know when I am in this place. All the uncertainty I feel is calmed. The anger and volatility tamped down into barely smoldering ashes.

"Please, God. Be with me, with us. Give me the words. Be my words." I silently pray, deep breaths in and out, in and out.

Brigham opens the door to join me.

Here we go …

"Do you want to join me?" I ask, opening my hand to the space next to me on the love seat.

"Sure."

I turn toward him as he sits down. He looks at me, gently cocking his head sideways in question of what's to come.

I smile uncertainly. *What do I say?* A small, nervous giggle floats up from my throat.

"What's up?" Brigham wonders aloud.

Deep breath.

"Well, I've been working a lot on some things and …" Another deep breath.

"Yes? And?" his words are gentle, encouraging.

"Well … there's more to the John story that I should tell you."

"Okay???" He is puzzled.

"So, it wasn't … He wasn't …" Breathe. "You know how he wasn't always nice to me?"

"Yes. I remember."

"Well, it was more than that. He was abusive." I turn my gaze from him to the crucifix on the wall. *Give me strength.*

"Okay?" his tone is both gentle and compelling. "What exactly does that mean?"

"He sexually abused me."

I look up, turning my eyes directly to this man with whom I've spent the past eighteen years. Eighteen years of less-than-the-whole-truth. Eighteen years of begging, groveling, fearing I would never be enough.

There is an immediate look of surprise, almost as quickly replaced by a sadness I haven't before seen on my husband's face.

"I am so, so sorry that happened to you." His compassion flows to me. "I am just horrified that would have happened to you."

I exhale a breath that carries an unfathomable weight. I let go of the tension I have held throughout my body for so very long, sinking back into the overstuffed cushions.

Tears roll slowly down his cheeks.

"I feel such an overwhelming sense of sadness. Growing up is supposed to be a fun magical experience of carefree child's play." His words tumble forward to comfort me.

"Yes …" I agree, my sadness echoing his. "Yes, it is."

"I'm not really sure what to do with this. I'm not sure what to say."

"It's okay," I share with surprising conviction because I'm realizing it *really is okay* …

"I guess this caught me by surprise. I don't understand," his words echo the confusion on his face, "How is this something that you kept secret for so long? How could your parents not know? How could you not tell them? How could it not be discovered? How was it not obvious?"

"It's not something I ever told anyone. And I'm not sure how no one knew, but they didn't. And that doesn't really matter anymore because here we are."

"When did this happen?" he asks.

"From when I was about eight until I was eleven."

He hangs his head in overwhelming grief.

"But you were just supposed to be a kid without a worry in the world," he mumbles. "I can't imagine … This must have added exponentially to an already difficult childhood with you constantly moving, and you were never able to feel a part of something … All that isolation … The loneliness …"

I am silent. Eerily still. *So, this is what it feels like? This is what I've feared all these years?*

"I want to scoop you up and hold you. Can I do that? I'm just not sure what to do here."

"There is nothing you can do," I respond with calm finality. "You can just be here with me."

"Okay … Okay …"

Silence fills the room. After so many years of yelling and aggression, the silence feels like a gentle, warm breeze. A hug between and around us both.

"Ugh!" Brigham grunts, interrupting the momentary quiet. "I'm just so very angry!!! Where is he? Do you know where he is now?" The words come flooding out like water through a fire hose. His strength—as my husband, as a military veteran, as the caring protector he is at his core—surrounds me.

"What about all those times he reached out over the years? And your family, wasn't it your aunt or uncle who kept in touch with him?"

"I don't know," I answer, "I just don't know."

"I want to know where he is. I want to know that he isn't a threat any longer."

The more he speaks, the safer I feel.

"I just hate this for you. I hate that this is something so bad that it not only continues to affect you, it also, to some extent, changed the trajectory of your life …."

The open-ended sadness and compassion in his words provide a bridge for me to cross. It's as if the black shroud that has covered me up to this point has been gently but thoroughly removed. Tears fall down my cheeks as I slide over from my side of the love seat to where my One sits. I curl up in his open arms, and he wraps me in all the love I never imagined possible.

ᚼ ෬ ෬ ෬ ᚼ

What I most feared in life ended up being the greatest gift. Rather than hearing my story and being repulsed and leaving—as I was almost certain he would do—Brigham loved me. Well. His caring and tenderness, supported by an equal amount of protection, opened the door for me to begin the healing process. For the next two decades, I had little stutter-starts and stops of saying the things out loud to safe people. I had advances and retreats. At times I was pretty ugly and unlovable, but Brigham stood by my side, covering me as only a kinsmen redeemer would or could, and he has loved me through the long process of discovery and recovery that has led me to this moment where I am boldly sharing my story with you.

PERFORMANCE *anxiety*

My husband has loved me through the long process of discovery and recovery that has led me to this moment where I am boldly sharing my story with you.

chapter ten

GRACE TO HEAL

Like wildflowers, you must grow in all the places people never thought you would.

LULAROE HEATHER MOUBERRY

When enough people had played "peek-a-boo" with my secret for me to know that at least some recognized the scar of abuse, I grew the courage to share it with a few safe people.

The response to my story from those safe people let me know that this was not a nothing. Not the tiny thing I had diminished and hidden and pretended was not a big deal, but a thing of significance that had deeply impacted my psyche and overshadowed my relationships.

I never fit the stereotype of an abused woman. Abused women were introverted and shy, shrinking from engagement with others. Loners. They were mousy. Wore sunglasses to hide behind. In movies and television, they are cast as broken and show weakness and fragility, but I did not resemble that woman at all. I was strong. I was extroverted and boisterous. I projected fearlessness. Confidence. I had masked my pain for so long that it had become part of me. I barely acknowledged that the hollow parts of me were empty because the vessel was too broken to hold any living water for long.

≼☙❧☙❧≽

Unlike many abuse survivors, my life didn't devolve into a life of prostitution or substance abuse. And I guess that would make me one of the lucky ones. But I don't think luck had much to do with it.

I had angels along the way. There were angels with skin on who showed up or stepped in on my behalf and ministered to me in my place of need. Those who knowingly or unknowingly, intentionally or by the grace of God showed up to protect, guard, defend, comfort, guide, and direct my steps. I didn't recognize them as my angels at the time, but hindsight and all that …

One of the really cool things about angels is they come into your life when you need them. God's timing. When you are broken, that's all you can see. The brokenness. My shame, guilt, suffering drove me. It was my road map. It was my armored vehicle against being seen. Because being seen would mean everyone would know. And despite all the counseling and work I'd done, I still wasn't in a place where I wanted anyone to see me. Not really see me. No one could be as damaged and dirty as I was. I had to hide, lest they find out and be repulsed and run. The Christian friends and people at church and everyone who had anything to do with me. They couldn't know. And then Lisa showed up.

On a trip to see friends in Texas, I felt a repeated, insistent call to meet with one of my safe people, Lisa.

"So, Lisa, do you know why I'm supposed to meet with you?" I almost begged as I sat in the booth across from her.

"Do *I* know? No. I don't. Do *you*?"

The restaurant noise echoed around us. Texas sports bars on Sunday afternoons are a cacophony of athletic enthusiasts.

"Uh. No. I just know I'm supposed to meet with you," I squinted through the bright sun shining in my eyes despite tinted windows.

"Well, let's just talk, and maybe Real Dad will let us know."

Real Dad. That's what Lisa calls God the Father. I like it. There's a lot to it, but that's her story. My not-so-typical self feels safe with Lisa. She is not typical too. I can just be me with her. No editing. Raw.

"I ruined Nationals for my swim team," I blurt out. *Where did that come from? I've never told anyone about Nationals. About him.*

Lisa just looks at me. There is no judgment. There is only calming patience. She waits for me to continue.

"I ruined it. My parents, not knowing about any of it, brought my abusive brother to Nationals, and I froze, and I ruined it."

"I think we know why you're here," Lisa proposed, her eyes squinting a smile behind bright, orange-rimmed glasses.

We spent a long time together that afternoon. The story of my Nationals shame poured out me like a newly tapped geyser.

Finally, Lisa responded, "You have to write that down. You have a story to tell, and you have to write it down."

"Okay?" I questioned. *Write it down? Me? I can't write. Remember Professor Young? I am not a writer.*

PERFORMANCE *anxiety*

"Find my friend, Bookie. She does these workshops called Release the Writer. I think there's a workshop coming up this fall. It's good. She's good. Find her and write it."

"Alrighty then." I took her orders. It was Lisa, after all. Jesus himself might as well have said it.

I went online and signed up for the next Release the Writer conference that very night. I had a story to tell …

The conference was everything Lisa said it would be. I came away with more than just the spark of the potential of overcoming. I came away encouraged by the power of helping others overcome and live in freedom. Despite all my insecurities and fears, I began to believe that it would be worth the pain and process of dredging up these memories and writing the thing down.

∽ ○3 ○3 ○3 ∽

As a recovering athlete, I do exceedingly well with a tangible goal. I have years of experience in being coached, so having directions for writing my story felt familiar, safe, and life-giving. As I began to write and tell more people my story, I began to have empathy. I gave myself permission to acknowledge what had been done to me and begin to have compassion for those who had something done to them too.

And then life happened. Or I let it happen. Because doing the hard thing doesn't always mean it's a smooth or consistent road. Deciding to tell my story brought more wounds out into the open. I returned to counseling, ultimately to be diagnosed with PTSD. I found another level of understanding and healing as I processed through long-buried memories, but I stopped writing altogether.

GRACE TO HEAL

⊰༄⊱⊰༄⊱

Time passed. Lots of time. I was working for Fellowship of the Sword, a ministry very close to my heart. Lisa being Lisa walks in one day and came straight over to my desk.

"Hey, Lisa!" I greet her.

"Hey yourself."

"What's up with you?" I ask.

"I've been wondering about the last time we talked …."

"Oh, you have, have you?" I wonder aloud.

"Yeah. So, we're saved by the blood of the Lamb and …?"

"Umm," I pause to consider.

"We're saved by the blood of the Lamb *and* …" she repeats.

"The word of our testimony?" I am unsure.

"We are saved by the blood of the Lamb *and* …" she is more insistent than before.

"The word of our testimony," I repeat.

Lisa demands more. "We are saved by the blood of the Lamb *and* …."

"**The word of our testimony!**" I state with determination and finality.

"Exactly."

I wait. When Lisa says something, you listen. Her words are few and thoughtful, and impactful.

"And?" I ask.

"Why aren't you writing your book?"

PERFORMANCE *anxiety*

"Umm ..." I am a child called out by a beloved teacher. "Umm ..."

I knew why I wasn't writing my book. Writing my book meant I would have to tell my parents. How could I tell them?! All my performing. All my being "the good girl." All of that would be thrown out the window, and I'd disappoint them more than anything and everything I'd ever done wrong. I could tell anyone else in the whole world my story, but not them. I didn't want to hurt them. I didn't want them to reject me. I didn't want them to discredit my memories or project a narrative on top of my story to explain it some other way.

> *Writing my book meant I would have to tell my parents ... I could tell anyone else in the world my story, but not them.*

They say the best way to solve a problem is to admit you have one, so I guess I had a problem. I didn't feel safe telling my parents. Admitting that to one of my closest friends was my first step.

I always thought my mom was the more approachable of my parents. Maybe because she's a girl, like me, or maybe because my dad was a physically large man with a deep, baritone voice and a pugnacious personality. Dad also traveled a lot for work, so being closer and more at ease with my mom may have resulted from spending many years together, often just the two of us. Regardless of the reasons why, I decided to tell my mom first. She'd be the easier one to tell. She'd be the safer one to tell.

"So, I've been volunteering in the Freedom Ministry at church ..." I kept my focus forward as I drove. If I didn't look at her, it made it easier.

"I know. That's great. I'm glad God is using you to help others," she encouraged.

"And I met with Beth Helton, one of the leaders for Freedom Ministry …" I stalled with details.

"Oh, how'd that go?" mom asked.

"Well. It went well." I stopped talking to focus on the traffic around me.

Mom and I have our deepest discussions in the car. It's away from the house and other people, and it's a space neither of us can escape. It's a place where we solve the world's problems and battle our battles.

"So, I think I finally know why I'm at Gateway and part of the Freedom Ministry team," I nervously rush my words.

"Really?" Mom wonders.

"Yeah, so Beth and I were talking, and she was explaining that there are a lot of trends for post-Kairos counseling and support … And they're going to form support groups for those … One of them is for childhood wounds, and one is for addiction, and one is for women survivors of sexual abuse."

"Wow. That's great. Gateway is so good at helping people. I'm glad you are part of that." Mom's voice is gentle, hopeful, encouraging.

"So, Beth and I were talking and, you know, I've been wondering why God wants me there and …."

"Yes?" Mom's voice continues to encourage me.

"Well … So … Beth is telling me about these new groups, and she gets to the group for survivors of sexual abuse and … Well … I just blurted out in the middle of her talking, 'That's why I'm here! That's my story!'"

There, I've said it. I've told her. I exhale as I pull the car into the store parking lot.

Silence. I swallow a thick heavy gulp. *Mom?*

Mom shifts in her seat to turn toward me. I look up and see tears in her eyes. Tears and confusion. My first thought is to comfort her. *I've hurt her, and I need to make it okay.*

"It's okay, Mom."

"No. No, it's not okay. But … I don't understand."

"I know. And it's okay. Because I never told you. I never told anyone, but now I need to. I need to tell because I believe God has called me to Gateway and Freedom Ministry so I can help other people," I blurted out with both insecurity and conviction. I force myself to talk, my faith guiding me and providing the strength I need.

"Can you tell me who? When?" my mom pleads.

I inhale. *God, please help me.* "It was John."

"*John?*" my mother's devastation is palpable. "*John?*" she wonders again. "But … when???"

"From the time I was about eight until middle school," I say softly, gently, wanting to limit her pain. "But it's okay. It's over now. I've done the work. I'm *doing* my work. It's okay. It's going to be okay," I rush, throwing out words, willing it to be alright.

More silence. Deep swallows.

"I'm sorry," my mom cries. "I'm so, so sorry."

"Thanks, Mom. Really."

"But you've been seeing someone? You're okay?"

"Yes, I've been seeing someone, but I'm not sure I'd say I'm okay …"

"But you've been seeing someone? Getting help?"

"Yes," now I'm the one who's confused.

"And it only happened then?"

"Yes," I feel myself pulling away, unsure of the change in her tone and questions.

"Well, if it happened that long ago, shouldn't you be over it by now?"

And that, my friends, is lesson number one in what not to say to an abuse survivor.

"No, Mom. No. I don't think that's something you ever get over."

Three years after telling my mom, my beloved friend and counselor threw me a curveball. As we discussed my relationship with the primary men in my life, Israel proposed I look inward for the root in some of the brokenness.

"Would you consider that your need to be in control and do things perfectly robbed your dad of his opportunity to love you, protect you? His right to be your dad?"

Wait. What? Come again?

"Your dad loves you. I guarantee his deepest desire is to protect you. And you're not telling him [about the abuse] robbed him of that chance. Your relationship is broken, in part, because you know that. Because you wanted so much for someone to protect you, for your dad to protect you, and you understand, deep down, that you prevented that by not telling him."

Well, that's a bunch of …

"I want you to consider it. Not that you were wrong for not telling because *you absolutely were not wrong*, but that your relationship with him is broken, in part, because of not telling him. Could you tell him and give him the chance to love and protect you now? Going forward?"

Telling my mom was hard enough. She's my mom. And my friend. *Tell my dad? Are you serious?!*

PERFORMANCE *anxiety*

I wrestled with what Israel said. *Did I struggle with trusting my father when I knew I'd kept such a secret from him? I was the one who couldn't be trusted. I was the one who kept the secret.* I prayed. A lot.

Three years later, I had finally healed enough to move myself and my book forward. Three full years. A lifetime of pain, suffering, secrets, and hiding doesn't just disappear overnight. I worked with counselors, ministers, and friends to slowly but surely peel the layers of the walls and lies I'd put up. EMDR (Eye Movement Desensitization and Reprocessing) was a large part of calming the triggers that, mostly unbeknownst to me, had been calling the shots.

I was more and more vulnerable with others about the surface-level details of what had happened to me. No one, other than my counselors, knew the darkest of details. Still, the shame and stigma became less and less as I brought what I'd experienced out in the open. I was ready to begin writing again, which meant I'd have to tell my dad …

≼ ೞ ೞ ೞ ≼

"So, Mom, I've been thinking …"

"Uh-oh," she giggled, "What now?"

It was one of our little games. Whenever I said, "I've been thinking," it usually meant either something exceptionally deep or an adventure. Either way, we both took the moment with lighthearted anticipation.

"Well, I think I'm ready to tell Dad."

"Oh." She paused long enough for me to continue.

"Yeah. I've gotten to the place where I need to tell him. I can't write this book until I do."

"Okay. If you think you're ready, then that's good."

"I was wondering if maybe I could come over and the three of us could have dinner one night, and then I could talk with him?"

"Sure. Just let me know what day you're thinking, and I'm pretty sure I can make that happen."

Mom reached over and grabbed my hand. She gave it a gentle squeeze. I felt a bit of relief and encouragement. This was my mom. This was the same woman who massaged the Rheumatoid Arthritis pain from my hips after almost every single swim practice. This was my friend. Her squeeze and gentle smile gave me all the strength I needed.

A few days later, I walked through my parent's front door.

"Hey, Dad," I smiled as I walked in.

"Hey, Buzz," my dad smiled back, calling me by the nickname he'd given me as a toddler.

I walked over and hugged him. His arms welcomed me, and the angst I had about what was to come ebbed slightly.

"What do ya' know?" he asked.

"Not much …"

Our conversation soon included my mother, and the three of us chatted about anything and everything. My mom served up one of my favorite meals, but I couldn't eat much for the anxious knot in my stomach.

"Hey, Dad," I began after the dishes had been cleared and the kitchen cleaned.

"Yeah?"

"I need to apologize to you."

"You do?" he sat upright in his chair, puzzled.

"Yeah … Yes, I do," I continued.

"Okay," he waited for me.

"I need to ask your forgiveness for not letting you be my dad, for not letting you protect me and care for me … Because when I was younger, John abused me … I never told you. I never told anyone until recently. And I'm sorry. I'm sorry I didn't give you the opportunity to love and protect me. I didn't let you be my daddy."

It was as if time stood still. My father said nothing. He didn't move. The stillness was not what I had expected. *What are you thinking? Are you okay?* All my fears flooded forward. I was more uncertain than I'd ever been.

Tick. Tick. Tick. The clock noted the minutes.

I raised my eyes to meet his.

Tick. Tick. Tick.

"Daddy?"

"I think I'm glad you didn't tell me until now," he said with an eerily calm voice, "Had I known then, I think I would've killed him."

Relief washed over me. *He's not angry with me.*

"I'm sorry that happened to you," his gentle words sent the limitless fears I'd entertained into an abyss.

"Can you forgive me?" the voice of a very small girl asked her very strong daddy.

He opened his arms to me, and I walked over. Without thought, I dropped to my knees to meet him in his chair. I rested my head in his lap, and he cradled me, gently stroking the top of my shoulders.

"It's okay. It's alright now."

༄ ☙❧❧ ༄

I am certain neither of my parents would have wished any suffering on me. I am almost as certain my father would not have literally killed John. One last certainty—however much suffering I endured—my father was spared a truth that may have killed him. My dad suffered his first heart attack when he was 32. He would suffer at least two more heart attacks in his lifetime (Mom and I speculate he had one more) and spend the last two decades of his life in a wheelchair as multiple sclerosis ravaged his body.

I'm not sure I believe the adage, "God will never give you more than you can handle," but this I do know; God will give you the strength, His strength, to walk through whatever life does throw at you. God can and will redeem the most horrible of traumas.

Perhaps things would have been vastly different for me if my parents had known. Certainly, they would have been. But then maybe I wouldn't be the person I am today, and maybe I'd have grown up without the father who loved me so very much. Either way, I'm glad I got to mend things with my daddy. It's amazing what uncovering the truth can do for your soul!

༄ ☙❧❧ ༄

PERFORMANCE *anxiety*

Three short years later, years of continued health struggles and decline for my sweet daddy, I received a phone call that would once again put a halt to my writing.

"Hi Mom," I answered the trill of my cell phone, "How's Dad today?"

"He … I don't understand … He agreed to …" her breath forced pained words through the phone.

"Mom?"

"I don't know why or when, but Dad agreed to a heart catheterization, and they went ahead and did it this morning …"

"Wait. What?" I'm flabbergasted. My father has absolutely refused this procedure time and again, fearing it would certainly kill him. "He agreed to what?"

"I know. I don't understand it either. We spoke with the doctor yesterday, and he and I were in agreement he would not have the procedure. Then this morning, I received a call from the nurse telling me your dad was in recovery and that the procedure had gone well, and they wanted me to come up to the hospital as soon as possible to discuss the results …"

My mom's voice trails off in angst and exhaustion. My father had been admitted to the hospital two days earlier, in the midst of the Covid-19 pandemic. Everything was on lock-down, and no one other than patients and medical personnel were permitted in the hospital. The fact that they were asking my mom to come to the hospital ASAP was more immediately concerning than the fact my father had agreed to a procedure he had definitively rejected for years.

"Okay, Mom." *Please, God, please.* "Deep breath. What else did they say? Anything?"

"No. Nothing. Just that he had the heart catheterization, and he was in recovery, and I needed to come up."

Please, God. Not yet. Don't let this be the end. Not now. Please.

"I'm on my way to the hospital. I'll call you as soon as I know more," she spoke in a controlled panic.

"I'm here, Mom. I'm right here. We can be on the road and to you as soon as we need to. Just let me know what the doctor says, and we'll go from there."

"Yes. Alright. I'll call you as soon as I know more." And with that, the call disconnected.

It's amazing how time stands still in moments like these. I pace around the house, praying, tidying the kitchen, praying some more. I force panic away, pleading for my daddy to be okay, knowing he is not, understanding he cannot be okay.

The jingle of my cell phone ringer interrupts my pacing.

"Hi, Mom. What do you know?"

"Dad's in recovery. The procedure itself went fine. I'm here with the doctor … 95% blockage … not good … I'll let you talk with him …" I can feel the utter sorrow in her words.

"Hello, Jackie," the doctor's calm voice greets me.

"Hi, Doc. So, can you tell me more definitively? He has 95% blockage. What does that mean?" I ask.

"I'm sorry … yes … 95% blockage … typically 24-48 hours …I'll give you back to your mom …"

What?! 24-48 hours?! No! No! Everything within me breaks. I force the tears aside. I must be there for my mom. My dad and I had long ago agreed I would take care of my mom after he died. *It is that moment. Now is that moment. God, please …*

"Mom?"

"Yes. I'm here." Her voice sounds strangely distant.

"Mom. I'm on the way. I'm getting the boys and making the arrangements, and I'm on my way in one hour," I plead with her, "Just hang on. We're coming."

"Okay. Yes. Just drive safely."

"Mom?"

"Yes?"

"I love you."

"I love you too …"

෴ଓଔଓ෴

God's grace and mercy covered all of us for the next five days. Defying the odds, my father stayed with us and coherent long enough for my mother, my husband and I, and our three boys all to say goodbye. We all got to tell my dad how much we loved him, and he was effusive with how much he loved each one of us.

And then he went home.

It all seemed too much, losing my father in the midst of a pandemic. There was no grand celebration of his life. There was no chance to mourn in a larger setting. We clung to one another with intensity and fierceness, and then we did the next thing, the only thing any of us had ever thought to do … we packed up my mom and all her things and moved her to Alaska to live with us. Together, we would find a way to grieve, to celebrate, to remember, and to heal.

GRACE TO HEAL

~ ෬෨෬ ~

Healing looks different for each of us. Sometimes it's about healing relationships. Other times it about healing deep, soul wounds. You may need time to recoup physically. Mental and emotional healing can take a very, very long time, and both require a ton of effort. That time and effort are always well spent.

Healing looks different for each of us.

Today I'm sitting in my home office in Alaska during a snowstorm. I prefer the cold to the heat. Days like today encourage me to stay in, drink warm drinks in front of the fire, spend time with a good book, or play games with family. Everything about it makes me feel cozy, safe, and calm. I can breathe in peace and serenity. Wounds, old wounds, are allowed rest and recover on days like today.

All too often, abuse forces you to be on high alert 24/7. The fight-or-flight response goes into overdrive, preventing any form of rest or recovery. Study after study confirms the potential for long-term psychological as well as physiological consequences of abuse, childhood abuse in particular.

I, like so many, have suffered through the all-too-common fallout of surviving abuse: heavy drinking and binge drinking, living with chronic health conditions since the abuse began, and walking through the darkest pits of depression and anxiety.[1]

What conditions may be triggered by childhood trauma? No one can say for certain right now, but childhood abuse certainly plays a significant role in the development of many conditions—especially neurological and autoimmune. I was diagnosed with Juvenile Rheumatoid Arthritis at age 8. I was diagnosed with Multiple Sclerosis at age 31. While no one can say for certain the abuse caused these, there is little doubt that the abuse is linked to their development.

It wasn't until I was in my forties that doctors diagnosed me with PTSD. That was 100% the result of the abuse. A direct cause and effect relationship. Did the PTSD cause the arthritis or MS? Again, no one can say for certain. For now, there are some definitive links to PTSD and fibromyalgia. Other conditions connected to ACEs may include heart disease, headaches, and migraines, lung cancer, chronic obstructive pulmonary disease (COPD), liver disease, depression, anxiety, and even sleep disturbances.[2]

Science has proven that we respond to stress with our bodies, not just our minds. When children are abused, their development is warped. They have higher rates of inflammation, depression, and metabolic disorders than those with a happy, healthy childhood. I am positive that my health conditions have been exacerbated by the effects of abuse in my childhood and young adulthood.

Your place to recover and heal may not be the same as mine. Sunshine and water may be your go-to. Or maybe you prefer hiking in the mountains, spa days, or a lazy day in a hammock with a very good book. Whatever it is, wherever you find "your place," take note of it. There you can step out of hiding, alone or with another. You can spread your arms wide or snuggle under a comfy quilt. There you can let down your guard and be. Just be. And breathe.

I am living proof that it is possible to be fully known and fully loved. God has loved me with an extravagant love. Brigham has loved me with an enduring, patient love. My children and parents have loved me with devoted love. My friends have loved me with a cherishing love. I am loved—I have always been loved, even when I didn't know how to recognize, accept, or receive it. God has given me the grace to heal, and He will give it to you, too.

ENDNOTES

1. https://www.ncbi.nlm.nih.gov/pmc/articles/PMC4302144/.
2. https://www.healthline.com/health/chronic-illness/childhood-trauma-connected-chronic-illness#What-the-research-says.

PERFORMANCE *anxiety*

*God has given me the grace to heal,
and He will give it to you, too.*

chapter eleven

LOVE THEM ANYWAY

Father, forgive them, for they know not what they do.
LUKE 23:34

Evil lurks in this world; make no mistake. It exists in the hearts of men, and some are sinister, malevolent even. Some, though, are not purely evil; just twisted and broken, corrupted by the effects of evil. Broken people operate out of their brokenness. In their warped state, they hurt other people. I cannot judge the motives of those who hurt me. I don't know if they were fully aware and choosing to abuse me with sadistic pleasure or if they truly did not know any different.

In my healing journey, I realize I have hurt people I love. Not with any malicious intent, but out of total ignorance. Lack of awareness. Selfish protection. Selfish preservation. Brokenness. Maybe those who hurt me didn't really mean to do so either.

When my eldest child turned 13, I had a moment where God shined a huge light in my heart and opened my eyes to this possibility.

PERFORMANCE *anxiety*

What evil would have had to have happened to my son for him to have behaved as John behaved? Made the choices John made. Did the cruel, unspeakable things John did.

One afternoon at my son's baseball game, I witnessed an interaction between a father and a son where the son didn't do something correctly in the father's eyes. This angry, overbearing father got in a fistfight with his son—right there in the dugout.

I was dumbfounded. It was awkward. Uncomfortable. Painful to watch.

In the days that followed, a thought flickered. Then emerged. Then grew in strength.

Of course, I was angry that a grown man would treat a child in such an abusive way. But it slowly dawned on me that somewhere the terribly painful behaviors and attitudes I witnessed from the man must have had a root cause.

It was like someone opened the blinds on a window. The light from heaven shone forth, and I thought, *Wow, if that level of inappropriate behavior is happening in public, what must be going on in that young man's life behind closed doors?*

If the boy was enduring that kind of abuse, what abusive behavior might he be exercising on someone else as an outlet?

The boy was about the same age as John was when he first began abusing me. I began to ponder what might have happened in John's world that could have twisted his young heart and made his behavior towards me acceptable in his eyes.

This was the *very first time* it dawned on me that maybe John had not been evil—but *broken*.

It wasn't like a revelation emerged; then, there was a process of thoughtful contemplation. It was more like a dawning—almost instantaneous. The moment I considered this possibility, my heart turned, and I was flooded with compassion that only God could have supplied.

In an instant, I no longer hated John. I didn't even know how to wrap my head around it—*I don't hate John.* I checked my heart. I had this love for him that displaced my revulsion. My anger. My fear. *How can this be?* I knew I had no power to do that. It was a miracle. ONLY God could perform that transformation.

God. His grace and His mercy. I had to borrow it to step into it. It was supernatural. I felt like Moses must have felt when he came down from the mountain with the ten commandments in his hand. I was sure I was glowing—shining too brightly to be bearable. It was that big.

I fell to my knees in wonder. Adoration. Receiving this gift that was beyond my comprehension.

I borrowed all the grace and mercy of heaven and sprinkled it all over John and that situation.

Forgiveness isn't a big enough word to describe what I stepped into.

I didn't forgive John as an act of my will. It was more like God revealed His forgiveness of John through me. I stepped into God's forgiveness. I wore it like a garment. A supernatural cloak of forgive.

I didn't possess that kind of capacity for forgiveness.

What John did to me was a total violation of who I was at my core, and I was not equipped to overcome that. I didn't have the resources to overcome that, let alone forgive it and all the messy consequences that resulted.

PERFORMANCE *anxiety*

I have heard preachers pray for eyes to see and ears to hear. Suddenly, I understood what they meant. God gave me His eyes. His ears. Even through a glass darkly, I was overcome with compassion and love for a broken child, warped and twisted. It was like I separated myself from his abuse of me. I stood as an observer, aware that there was much to the story I did not know. Would never know. And it didn't matter.

I was free.

Free from the hate.

Free from the fear.

Free from the loathing. The revulsion. The anger.

Free.

I still had work to do because of the repercussions of choices I had made in the aftermath of John's actions to me. My circumstances did not change one bit. But I changed.

It was huge.

The venom I had in my heart towards John was gone—in a miraculous instant—which opened the door for my healing to begin. I was no longer gripped by the hatred and anger I had for him.

I breathed an echo of the prayer of Jesus, "Father, forgive John. Maybe he didn't really know."

❧ ୪୪୪୪ ❧

Then there was mom.

I didn't blame my mom. At least I didn't mean to blame my mom.

It never occurred to me that any of it was her fault. I know it happened on her watch, so at some level, I guess she was complicit. But she didn't know. She wasn't responsible for what John did to me.

When I first told her about it, it was unthinkable.

It wasn't that she didn't believe me or validate my experience; she just could not comprehend how it could have happened without her knowledge.

My mom was supermom.

Before there was such a thing as "helicopter moms," my mom was one.

At the tender age of twenty-seven, after miscarriages and a near-death birth, she opened her heart and her home to an eight and nine-year-old half-brother and sister. She had wanted to adopt a baby, but when she learned these children were without a home, knowing absolutely nothing about their health or history, she said, "I have so much love to give—bring them here!"

I always assumed they adopted them because I wasn't enough. Because I wasn't a boy. This was a lie that wrapped itself so tightly around my identity I still fight it. In truth, it was because I was so much to my parents—so much joy, so much delight, so much promise—that they wanted to have more children. They had always wanted a big family, and adoption was the only option for that dream to be fulfilled.

I think somewhere deep down, something in my subconscious blamed my mom. At some level, I was hurt that I was not protected.

> *This was a lie that wrapped itself so tightly around my identity I still fight it.*

I try to remember that it was 1973. We lived in a traditional Christian community, and there was very little knowledge and precious few resources for a young twenty-seven-year-old mother to cope with taking on two very troubled children.

PERFORMANCE *anxiety*

Our faith community was rigid. There was only one way to do things—God's way. (Well, at least how they interpreted God's way to be.) My mother strove to do "it"—whatever "it" was—the right way. She wanted to create a happy childhood for us.

Conversations with mom about my childhood have been hard. Painful. More intense because my father has now passed from this world to the next, and mom has come to live with us in Alaska. All the emotion of losing him has piled onto the emotion of realizing my childhood was not as happy or as healthy as she believed has been a huge blow.

I'm proud of her.

I'm proud that she has let me use my voice. Let me speak. Let me cry. Let me struggle to find my way through the fog and reclaim my lost identity.

I realize my story takes her entire life's experience as a parent and throws in a giant "BUT." With tears brimming from her brilliant blue eyes, she has grappled with, "How did I not know? How could I not know? How could this *possibly* be?"

She was a good mom. Involved. Attentive.

Mom has never doubted my story, but there was an incomprehensible moment that this could not possibly have happened on her watch. She was so engaged that it seemed inconceivable that this could have possibly escaped her notice.

It was 1973. Sure, we knew about creepy pedophiles. We knew about stranger danger. We never in a million years thought about young boys we knew being inappropriate with our girls. This level of depravity had not yet entered our culture's consciousness. There was no education for recognizing the signs of sexual abuse.

John was crafty. Careful. He hurt me in secret, and he exercised enough control to keep me silent and afraid. "Children should be seen and not heard" kept me from opening my mouth. "Wiersmas don't complain" kept me from seeking the protection I so desperately desired.

The eyes of a child. The perspective of a child. The silent pain of a child.

Just as I did when I forgave John by stepping outside of myself, I finally stepped out of being my mother's daughter. When I did this, it occurred to me that I didn't need to somehow prove my worth to my mother so she could love me unconditionally. I was enough, after all.

God allowed me the gift of heaven's perspective so I could borrow that same grace, mercy, and love to love her unconditionally—exceedingly, abundantly more than she had ever dreamed or imagined.

And I do.

I do not blame my mother. Instead, I have heartfelt compassion for the little girl's mother who had this horrible thing happen to her.

I weep with her.

More freedom.

More forgive.

⁂

So, what about my dad?

I must say, what I am about to tell you doesn't even seem fair to me.

I never ever blamed my dad.

Never.

PERFORMANCE *anxiety*

I never held him responsible in any way because he was never around.

Dad was busy being the businessman. He was the provider. Gone. Doing important things so we would have a roof over our heads and clothes in our closets and food on our table.

Dad was much less involved in caretaking than mom. So it never occurred to me then or now that he should have seen anything because he wasn't ever there to see.

That is a huge burden my small self put on my mom.

As a mom of three boys, I look back and realize how underwater she must have been to go from one child to three in an instant. John and Dori were a handful from the get-go.

I never blamed my dad. Mom, I'm sorry I blamed you. I want to tell you this:

I get it. I don't know how you did it. I don't know how you survived it. It feels so awesome to think that you did survive it. You brought these two children into our home out of love. You took them on without any additional skills or support to navigate their turmoil and trauma, and you gave it your all. You desperately tried to love them into love.

How could you possibly take that perfect, all-encompassing love you had and cover brokenness that you have never experienced, never witnessed, no one had discussed, no had prepared you for? This was not like warming a bottle or putting a diaper on—this was taking on two broken children with a long history of something you didn't know and couldn't imagine.

I don't know how you did it.

It was an epic battle for which you had no armor and no training. It was like fighting the Huns with an apron and a toothbrush.

That you and daddy survived as a loving couple, that the three of us came out on the other side of all that trauma and drama intact, is a miracle.

The words, "Mom, I forgive you," do not feel like enough.

I just want to hug you.

A proper hug.

The kind that conveys heart and soul, breath and life, understanding and awareness of what cannot be understood.

Mom, I just want to love you well.

I want you to be free from the burden of this knowledge and the great weight of care it has brought to you.

There is nothing else that needs to be done. There are no more words that need to be exchanged. No motives to be measured.

Nothing.

You are enough now. You were enough then.

I love you well.

You have loved me well.

Between us, all is well.

✧ ೫೫೫ ✧

There is no space for anything else when you are just trying to survive. Thrive is not even possible. It is like telling someone who has always known that the earth is flat that it is round.

It is inconceivable. It is heresy.

PERFORMANCE *anxiety*

The lies of others and the lies you learn to tell yourself are the fuel that powers the survive engine. It is the Catechism of your survive religion.

Sometimes, we whittle away at the lies in microscopic chips, and sometimes we drop an atom bomb on them. But as long as survive is the reigning deity of our mind, we cannot escape its long finger of accusation and reformation.

You are faithful to the law of survival. Freedom is sacrilegious, and even approaching it brings terror and guilt.

This is why living in freedom is so passionate for me. It is why I am open to the wise counsel of others even when I hate what they have to say. They demolish the arguments of that false survival religion, and in doing so, I have learned that I am loved because people love me enough to pull me out of that darkness.

Real love confronts everything that stands between you and the love of God.

Even when that thing is yourself and your ideology.

Even when that thing is your right to victimhood.

Even when that thing is brokenness for which you are not responsible.

Real love gets to the heart of the matter and beckons you into the light of truth, no matter what dark night you must pass through to breach the dawn.

Ultimately, there have been so many woulda coulda shoulda moments, and hindsight is 20/20. Forgiving others is a slam dunk. The Bible is full of counsel on forgiving others.

Forgiving myself is harder.

But because God forgives me, I don't have to do that work. Just like I did with John and my mom, I just get to step into it. His love. His grace. His mercy. His forgive.

I just have to step into God's forgiveness of me and learn how to cloak myself in that acceptance and peace. He has done all the work for me. My portion is to receive.

Simply receive.

Jesus said, "Father, forgive them." He put no condition on it.

So neither should I.

I can't perform my way perfectly into His forgiveness. He gives it out of His goodness, not because of mine.

His forgiveness included Judas—who absolutely *knew* He was betraying Jesus. With intent. With motive. With reward.

But did Judas *really* know what He was doing?

What was His story? How did Judas get to that place where He would betray *Jesus* for a few coins?

Maybe Judas didn't really know.

Maybe John didn't know either.

Even if he was aware that what he did to me was wrong or harmful, maybe he had no idea *why* he was capable of doing it. I'm sure he had no concept of the lifelong consequences to me … to him.

Either way, I pray, "Father, forgive him. He knew not what he did."

If John were ever to read this book, I would say to him:

What happened to you in the first nine years of your life that opened the door for that kind of depraved twist? What lies wrapped around your young heart and placed there this need to exercise control.

PERFORMANCE *anxiety*

To dominate.

To hurt someone and derive pleasure from that harm.

What demons lurked in your closet?

Are you sorry? Would you take it back?

How did what you did to me impact you for the rest of your life?

Did you ever have a daughter?

Did you worry that someone would do to her what you did to me? Did you protect her?

Did you ever even once look at me as a sister, or was I never that, to begin with?

Did you feel pressure to be a perfect, golden child like I did? Was it worse because you were also the "only son," the heir? Was I a threat to you somehow?

Was that why you hurt me?

Have you met Jesus?

Do you feel sick sitting here with me now the way I feel sick sitting here with you?

John, I'm really sorry for whatever happened to you—I'm so, so very sorry.

I don't hate you. I think I actually love you.

That's God.

Only God could work that miracle. Only God could allow compassion to arise and replace revulsion. Hope to shroud shame.

I hope whatever torment exists in your world; seeing me and talking to me now could give you some modicum of peace.

LOVE THEM ANYWAY

Go in peace, John. Go in peace.

Be free.

PERFORMANCE *anxiety*

Forgiveness says, "You're not important enough to have a stranglehold on me."

It's saying, "You don't get to trap me in the past. I am worthy of a future. I am moving on to peace and happness.'"

JODI PICOULT

chapter twelve

WALKING IN FREEDOM

Freedom is what you do with what's been done to you.

JEAN-PAUL SARTE

Patterns are easy. Habits are easy. Living on autopilot is easy. But there is so much more to life than just going through the motions without much thought or effort. When I first began doing the soul work for healing to bring about positive change, it required tremendous energy. As an athlete, physical effort was very familiar. This was different. The mental and emotional exertion were a big lift. The spiritual engagement seemed daunting. It would have been easier just to do things the way I'd always done them, good or bad, right or wrong; it would have been easier.

Digging deep into the hows and whys of my thoughts and actions provided plenty of opportunity for growth. I spent many hours and days and then weeks, even months peeling back the layers of hurt and lies and wrong thinking. Every step was hard, and every step has been worth the effort. Truly.

I learned a lot about myself as a person and even more about how I relate to others. The abuse survivor can come away with some pretty messed up filters, and I was a top-of-the-class example. Understanding myself, my triggers, and my potential pitfalls has been instrumental in moving forward for me. I am able to walk in freedom because I've done the work. I continue to do the work. I hope some of what I've learned and the tools I use can help you as well.

Patterns and habits do not disappear with a decision. They are deeply engrained in your psyche. Responding in different ways to familiar triggers takes great awareness, intentional replacement of routines, and accountability. It takes grace when you slip and courage to renew your mind. Freedom is more of a process than it is a place.

Here are some of the tools I have found helpful to keep me in the place where I can boldly and securely say I am living in freedom!

TAKE EVERY THOUGHT CAPTIVE

When I am challenged in my thoughts, I say, "Jesus!" He is the ripcord on the parachute as my thoughts overtake me and my mind spins, only focusing on the torment and lies it knows all too well. His name stops the terror of the fall and lets me glide down in safety back to a place of solid footing. Jesus removes the fear. He removes the danger. He is Psalm 91. There are times when I silently call out His name once or twice, and the angst subsides. Other times it will take one minute, or five, or fifteen minutes. Regardless, I know that His name will bring peace, and I intentionally keep it close in my arsenal against my demons.

Other times, when my thoughts are being less-than-helpful, I meditate. Meditation can take many forms and isn't limited to a faith-based exercise. Transcendental meditation is another method I've used to urge myself into a calmer, more peaceful state. At the essence of meditation is choosing to focus your attention so acutely that other things recede to the background. Even a few minutes can make a big difference in bringing your thoughts back into a place of calm order.

BREATHE ON PURPOSE

Another great tool is something I learned from my high school swim coach. Focused breathing forces a racing heart and unchecked breathing into a calm(er) state.

"Our breath can significantly change the state of our mind. So usually, if we're in a very high-stress moment, it's very difficult to talk ourselves out of it. It's just very challenging to change your mind with your own mind, your thoughts with your own thoughts. However, if you calm your nervous system, which is what we do with breath, then your mind can start to calm down as well."[1]

Here is a memory about breath from my swimming days:

It's early. Too early. But this is what I do. Morning practice is part of the routine, and, lucky for me, today is one of the morning practices where we learn how to relax. I don't quite understand all the "flex your feet as tight as you can and then release it" drills, but it means I don't have to be up at 0-dark-thirty and in the jarring cold of the pool so I'm game.

The lights are low through the hallway and in the gym as we climb the stairs to the mat storage room above. One by one, we grab red gym mats and spread them across the floor. No one speaks. It is a small attempt to stay half-asleep.

I flop onto the mat in front of me. There is no grace in it, just the desire to lay down and relax.

"Alright, girls, let's get settled. You know what to do …" Scott speaks just loud enough to focus us on the task at hand. No need to shout up here in the dark quiet.

"Let's start with your feet … Flex as hard as you can. Hold … Now relax."

The same drill is repeated, progressing upward through the legs, the stomach, the shoulders. After we have flexed and relaxed every muscle he identifies, we move on to breathing.

"Deep inhale through your nose … two, three, four. Hold, two, three … six, seven. Exhale, two, three … six, seven, eight."

We repeat the breathing drill again and again. Some of my teammates fall asleep. Some are restless. I sink into the space between sleep and awake. Nothing is in focus, save for the fact this is one of the very few times and places I let my guard down and rest. No competition. No performance.

Here I let go and breathe. I am calm.

Letting go isn't always easy. The need to perform doesn't always come in expected and rational moments. Sometimes a need to be perfect and fix "everything" plagues my mind. My thoughts race like a runaway train, especially at night. I routinely use focused breathing to settle into sleep when, as my husband says, "I am saving the manatees."

I want to encourage you to be patient when trying focused breathing. You may not be able to breathe in for 4, hold for 7, and exhale for 8. That's okay. Start where you can. Keep at it. Even the smallest of efforts can afford help.

GO GREEN

I get out in nature. When four walls feel like a prison, I take my thoughts captive, as if on a leash, and walk them to God along a path or trail. Scientific research has proven that being out in nature reduces fear, anxiety, anger, and stress. It increases feelings of well-being and pleasure. Studies show time outdoors reduces blood pressure, slows your heart rate, relaxes muscle tension, and lowers the production of stress hormones like cortisol.

I love that there is research, but I don't need the research to tell me that the closer I am to creation, the closer I am to the Creator. I hand Him the captive thoughts and let Him take them.

KNOW WHO'S REAL

You know that your thoughts aren't real, right? At least not all of them. That condemnation you hear over and over again, it's not God. God does not condemn. He does not tell you that you're not good enough. He doesn't criticize you. Those thoughts; they are not real. They are not truth.

So very often, the lies overtake the abuse survivor. So very often, they overtake me.

You are not enough. You can't. You get what you deserve. It's your fault. You will never be enough.

Identifying the thought condemning me, harassing me, or bringing me anxiety or stress allows me to box it off. I am not that thought, merely the observer of that thought. Thus, I have the power to reframe that thought or even completely replace it with truth I have come to know and keep at the ready. Having some affirmations on hand is incredibly helpful when the emotions of a moment cause my mind and body to panic.

You are more than enough. You are resilient and strong. You are fearfully and wonderfully made. Your future is bright. You are accepted. You are loved.

Maybe your lies are different. Maybe not. Either way, I now know that it is important to find someone or a few someones to tell you the truth. To tell you who is real. The lies aren't real. They aren't truth. God is real. His love is real. His love for you is real.

BE KIND

I surround myself with other godly women. Those who speak God's truth with love. Those who are kind, not (necessarily) nice. There is a marked difference between nice and kind. Nice is hospitable. Nice is polite. Nice would never say anything to ruffle your feathers. Kind speaks the truth in love. Kind says, "I love you enough to tell you the truth, even if it's hard." Kind will call you out – gently – when you've missed the mark. Kind encourages you to be the best you.

BE PRUDENT

I stay away from being alone with men who are not my husband, recognizing I have some old habits and thoughts and issues that may skew how I see and expect men to see me.

Let's be incredibly raw for a second.

Abuse writes a very convincing equation: sex = love.

We've already discussed that craziness. What I want to call out here is that those deep ruts in the survivor's psyche can be formidable. It isn't a conscious or intentional act. Viewing others or expecting them to view you in a sexual manner is part of the baggage. And when you believe your interactions are sexualized, your thoughts too often become your reality. It's something that took me a long time to understand. Learning and accepting that you can work with, socialize with, and interact with members of the opposite sex and keep them in the "friend zone" is a good and healthy thing.

BOUNDARIES ARE WISE.

Do you know that line in *When Harry Met Sally*, "Men and women can't be friends"? Let me tell you; abuse survivors believe that to their core. I believed that to the very center of my being. It was and is a complete lie, but there you have it.

I've had a couple of significant men in my life prove otherwise. Their attitudes and actions (or lack thereof) confused me at the time. It made no sense to me that a guy would want to be just friends. That I had anything to offer beyond sex. Looking back, I know they were laying the groundwork for a healthy relationship between us.

PERFORMANCE *anxiety*

Imagine the irony of being an abuse survivor and being a swimmer. You learn that sex equals love. You learn that you are only valued as a sexual being. And then you spend the better part of your life surrounded by boys and men in itsy bitsy tiny Speedos. Good golly. Talk about a recipe for disaster!

It's really easy to flirt when everyone is all but naked. My teammates—men and women—must have thoughts I was—well, I'm not sure what they thought—but I have a lot of not-so-wonderful thoughts about myself and my actions when I look back.

Luke, one of the guys on the Miami Men's swim team, was my first introduction to men and women as friends. He was textbook good-looking. He was engaging. He was bright. And he never crossed the line into even the slightest flirtation. I'm sure I flirted with him. That was my modus operandi. Still, though he stayed engaged, he didn't return any flirtation, neither did he avoid me. His behavior was compelling and confusing at the same time. Somewhere he laid the seed of "just friends" that would continue to grow.

Many years later, one of Mac's dearest friends and I had a life-changing conversation.

"You know why you always felt safe around me, Jackson?" Harrison asked.

"No," I laughed. *What could he be talking about?*

"You always felt safe around me because I was the only one of Brigham's friends who didn't want to sleep with you."

I swear a lightbulb went off in my mind. Epiphany. This lifelong friend summed up what I didn't even realize, let alone understand so clearly. He *was* safe. *I* was safe. Once again, my spidey-sense had told me something for which I had no words nor experience. I finally began to understand the difference. Men and women *could* be friends.

I want to caution you strongly here. Set solid boundaries. Married, dating, or single, be mindful of the anchor that can drag you into old, lie-filled patterns. You are more than sex. Much more. And for goodness' sake, do not "friend" an ex on social media. It's far too easy to rekindle a rosy (and often false) memory of a relationship when things are not perfect in your current one.

Keep your guard up. Protect your heart and mind.

BE A SUPERHERO

I honor my spidey-sense and steer clear of unsafe men and situations. It isn't always obvious to me, let alone others, but if something or someone feels "off" to me, I respect that sense. For a long time, I dismissed what I couldn't logically explain. My deep need to do things "the right way" for others too often overrode my needs in an uncomfortable or dangerous situation. I've learned to value myself enough to walk away.

I ask those in my life who care about me to honor my spidey-sense—even if it does not make sense to them. "Hey, I'm sure you didn't mean anything inappropriate by _____, but because of my wife's (sister's/daughter's) history, things like this make her feel unsafe. Please refrain from _____ behavior around her." This allows for them to know the behavior is not okay without accusing them.

PAY IT FORWARD

I want to create opportunities for girls and women who have endured the horror of sexual abuse to gain freedom—and sooner rather than later. I want to give them the ability to use their voice, find places of safety, and begin to work through the trauma and damage.

I want to heighten the awareness of the community to create places of trust and safety for our little girls and big girls to be able to share when they feel unsafe and know that they will be respected, loved, and protected. The first step in the process is to make sure girls know someone who can say, "You have the ability to talk to me about anything. I am a safe place for you. I will never belittle what you feel or experience, and we'll find a way to work through it together."

God will make all things beautiful in its time. I honor the dark part of my story. I redeem it because I have submitted it to God's grace, been washed in the cleansing, healing blood of the Lamb, and I have applied that blood to my testimony. I have overcome!

Friends, I invite you to "Live in freedom!"

ENDNOTE

1. Emma Seppälä, author of *Happiness Track* and director of the Center for Compassion and Altruism Research and Education at Stanford University.

photo gallery

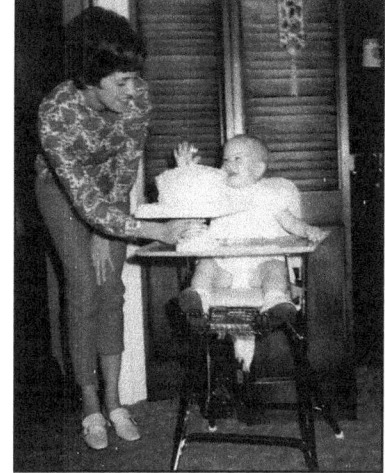

Joyful, happy years before Dori and John joined our family.

"Bikini Girl!"   Jackie and her neighborhood "Biker Gang."

PERFORMANCE *anxiety*

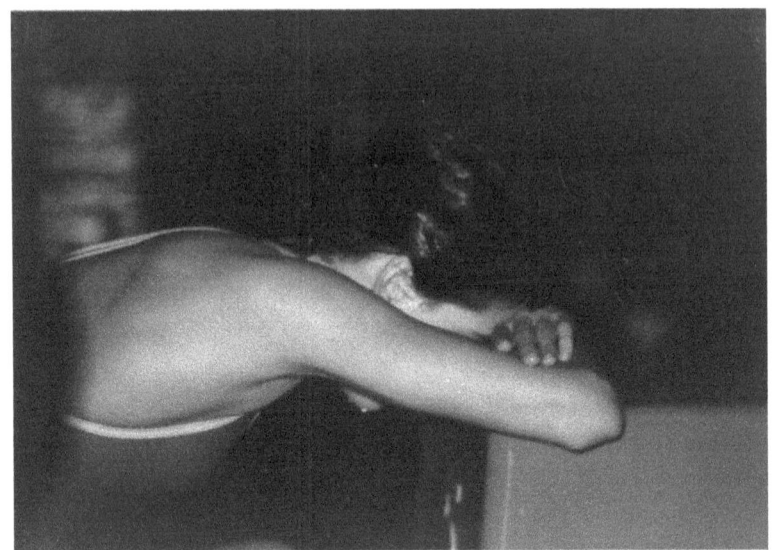

The agony of defeat ...

Jackie and Dad—the original Jackson.

PHOTO GALLERY

Jackie and Bonnie enjoying a moment between events.

Jackie & Mom celebrating Carnivale.

The Mac. My Mac.

Welcome to the Navy, Mrs. McCown.

Mom. Daughter. Friends.

PHOTO GALLERY

20th Anniversary Vow Renewal, Loch Lomond, Scotland.

Jackie & the Mac hiking in Montana.

PERFORMANCE *anxiety*

My happy place ...

PHOTO GALLERY

Jackie & the Mac at Mt. McKinley.

Coach!

PERFORMANCE *anxiety*

Reaching through the past to help others in their present.

It's okay—you are not alone.

about the author

JACKIE McCOWN

Jackie McCown captivates audiences with messages of hope and courage that inspire and empower them to overcome challenges and break free from performing for approval. Whether serving as a motivational speaker, a freedom coach, or training others to walk women through abuse recovery, Jackie draws on many years of personal experience, helping people find freedom.

Author of *Performance Anxiety*, Jackie loves to share insights based on real-life situations and easy to apply principles. She was diagnosed with Multiple Sclerosis in 2001 but has still run a marathon, two half marathons, and completed a 150-mile bike ride to raise money for research. A nationally ranked swimmer at Miami University and Division 1 scholarshiped athlete, Jackie

is a survivor of both childhood and adult sexual abuse. She knows first-hand the trauma this brings. After years of guilt, shame, and performing to please everybody, Jackie has learned to find purpose beyond performance.

In her own journey to find freedom, she has received training specific to addressing these issues. She has a passion for seeing others experience and walk in freedom from things that have constrained them. Jackie now serves as the Director for the Fellowship of Female Athletes, a support organization for women.

www.ingramcontent.com/pod-product-compliance
Lightning Source LLC
Chambersburg PA
CBHW070542090426
42735CB00013B/3053